Scribe Short Books
51ST STATE?

DENNIS ALTMAN is Professor of Politics at Latrobe University.
The author of eleven books, including *Gore Vidal's America*,
Global Sex and the memoir *Defying Gravity*, he was Professor of
Australian Studies at Harvard (2005), and has held visiting
fellowships at New York University (2002) and University of
Chicago (1997). He has served on a range of international
committees on HIV/AIDS, and served as president of the AIDS
Society of Asia and the Pacific between 2001 and 2005. He was
named by the *Bulletin* in June 2006 as one of the 100 most
influential Australians ever.

SCRIBE SHORT BOOKS

concise perspectives on important developments
in society, culture, and politics

General Editor: Russ Radcliffe
russradcliffe@scribepub.com.au

IN THE SAME SERIES

Don't Tell the Prime Minister
Patrick Weller

Western Horizon
David Burchell

Howard's War
Alison Broinowski

Orwell's Australia
Dennis Glover

Herzl's Nightmare
Peter Rodgers

Reluctant Saviour
Clinton Fernandes

Don't Think of an Elephant!
George Lakoff

The Still-Burning Bush
Stephen Pyne

Fear and Politics
Carmen Lawrence

51st State?
Dennis Altman

Reluctant Indonesians: the future of West Papua
Clinton Fernandes (October 2006)

51ST STATE?

DENNIS ALTMAN

SCRIBE SHORT BOOKS
Melbourne

Scribe Short Books is an imprint of
Scribe Publications Pty Ltd
PO Box 523
Carlton North, Victoria, Australia 3054
Email: info@scribepub.com.au

First published by Scribe 2006
Copyright © Dennis Altman 2006

Typeset by the publishers in 11/16pt Minion
Cover image courtesy of Photolibrary
Printed and bound in Australia by Griffin Press

National Library of Australia
Cataloguing-in-Publication data

Altman, Dennis, 1943- .
  51st state?

ISBN 1 920769 98 6

1. Social contract. 2. Australia - Civilisation - American
influences. 3. Australia - Relations - United States. 4.
United States - Relations - Australia. 5. Australia -
Politics and government - 2001- . I. Title.
(Series : Scribe short books).

303.48294073

www.scribepub.com.au

Contents

E·PLURIBUS·UNUM

Australia Welcomes America

Postcard commemorating the arrival in Australia of the Great White
Fleet in August 1908.

Introduction

We live in a world dominated by the American imaginary. We watch American television and movies, we wear clothes emblazoned with American emblems, we follow the lives of American celebrities. 'Making it' now usually involves being embraced by the United States, and a long line of entertainers and sportspeople have followed earlier Australians, such as Errol Flynn and Peter Finch, to New York and Hollywood. That Rupert Murdoch, Kylie Minogue, Nicole Kidman, and Russell Crowe are now global media figures is evidence of the ways in which smart Australians can take advantage of an increasingly globalised entertainment and commercial world. But there should be no illusion that trans-Pacific exchanges are anything but lopsided. One Australian count of 'the ten most memorable TV events from the last 50 years' listed five US events (numbers one and two on the list were the World Trade Center bombings and the moon landing) and only two Australian (Whitlam's rage after his sacking and the inquest into the disappearance of Azaria Chamberlain).[1]

To many Australians our very identity and sovereignty as a

nation is threatened by the growing influence of the United States. In 2005 the historian Jim Davidson wrote: 'Australia … is drifting into a situation where it is technically sovereign, but increasingly inseparable from America in both foreign and domestic policy, given the Free Trade Agreement … the republic we're headed for will probably be a latter-day version of the Texan Republic'.[2] For many Australians the major changes to industrial relations subsequently introduced by the Howard government bore the further marks of American influence. At the same time, the French government made changes to their industrial relations laws which were less far reaching than those simultaneously being implemented in Australia, but which unleashed a wave of protests, marches, and demonstrations that forced the government to abandon the changes. The contrast with the muted public responses in Australia, despite strong protest from the unions and the federal opposition, and immediate reports of sackings and significant cuts in wages and conditions, is striking.

Even if the government were influenced by American models in industrial relations, we cannot blame the United States for the mildness of the ensuing reaction. There is a mood of timidity and passivity in contemporary Australian political life, but its roots are to be found in ourselves, not in external influences. Indeed, the tendency to attribute American influence to everything we dislike about contemporary Australia is the mirror image of seeing the United States as a model to be emulated. In arguing the proposition that we are becoming 'inseparable from America' there is a larger challenge

— namely, how does Australia imagine its future? The United States offers one model, but there is no pre-ordained linear progression that means we must necessarily become more like them. As the writer John Birmingham asserted: 'Australia is not a colony, or a branch office, or the fifty-first state of the United States'.[3]

Yet Australian prime ministers since Harold Holt, with the partial exception of Gough Whitlam and Paul Keating, see a highly publicised visit to the White House as the ultimate accolade. Since the election of John Howard's government in 1996 there has been a series of initiatives to link us more closely to the US politically, militarily, economically, ideologically, and culturally. The United States has honoured Howard more than any previous prime minister: in August 2005 he became the first person outside the North-Atlantic world to receive a public service award from the Woodrow Wilson International Centre, at a dinner in Sydney to which President George W. Bush sent a recorded message of congratulations. That John Howard gets one fleeting reference in David Hare's play about the Iraq war, *Stuff Happens*, is probably a more accurate assessment of our importance in Washington; nonetheless, contact between the two governments is widespread, constant, and involves a fair degree of mutual trust. The expansion of an Australian military presence, which currently extends from Iraq in West Asia through to the Solomons in the Pacific, has meant closer and more complex links with the American military, security, and diplomatic establishment than at any time since World War II.

There is a widespread perception that Australia is being

'Americanized' (and here I adopt, deliberately, the American rather than the British spelling), in which one hears echoes of the larger debate as to whether globalisation is equivalent to Americanization, and in turn whether anti-Americanization becomes, therefore, a surrogate for hostility to 'the modern'.[4] This is not a new complaint; during the Gold Rush of the 1850s an American hotelier in Melbourne boasted, 'You will be surprised to see how fast this place is being Americanised …'[5] European observers often commented on the similarities, seeing Australia as sharing the brashness but also the egalitarianism of Americans.[6]

The claim that Australia is losing its political and cultural sovereignty to the United States has re-emerged, perhaps in sharper tones, at the beginning of this century. In 2001, in his influential *Quarterly Essay*, 'Rabbit Syndrome', named after the central character in John Updike's series of novels of American middle-class angst, Don Watson suggested this was happening — 'so long as the little things that feed the soul, from Nike to the news, come straight out of the American blender, more and more of our days will be filled like Rabbit's' — and argued, though ironically, that Australia should recognise the inevitable and petition to join the United States.[7] Given that this was not the first time the possibility has been floated — though never, as far as I know, seriously — I was surprised to discover that *51st State* has not been more invoked as a title. There are several satirical novels which have used the term, and it surfaces in political discussion from Taiwan to Panama.

Labor politician Wayne Swan recently wrote:

4

Our politics are coming to resemble those of the United States … as we become more socially divided, we're becoming more politically divided. As the social democratic safety nets of our society disappear; as prosperity becomes less secure and the consequences for families of losing prosperity become more catastrophic; and as postcodes become a greater barrier to shared citizenship, it's becoming easier to appeal to people's fear and self-interest rather than promote the common good.[8]

Swan's analysis was echoed by sociologist Peter Beilharz, who wrote that Australia was adopting 'the Hollywood style of politics, where leadership is more often reactive and managerial rather than innovative or creative'.[9] It may seem odd to associate those qualities with Hollywood, but the reference is clearly to US-style campaigns. And recently the writer David Williamson spoke of travelling on a cruise ship, where, 'like Australia at large, no Australian song was ever played, no Australian movie ever shown, the trivia quizzes were all about American movie stars and we were offered Stetsons and boot-scooting'.[10]

The perception of 'Americanization' is often conflated with concerns about Australia's closeness to American military and foreign policy. During the Vietnam War concerns that Australia was becoming an American colony were often expressed within the anti-war movement, even though the weight of evidence suggests the Australian government had made its own assessment about the conflict, and used Australian troop commitments to encourage the Americans to increase theirs.[11] Equally, the establishment of American military installations in the period — at North West Cape (1967), Pine Gap (1969), and Nurrangar (1970) — seemed to many, including some of Whitlam's ministers, to symbolise an unnecessary dependence upon the United States, and one that increased rather than diminished the risk of Australia being attacked. Those bases remain, and there is virtually no pressure to remove them.

I think the decision to send troops to bolster an unpopular government in South Vietnam was a tragically wrong judgement, but that is different from asserting that the government *only* acted because of United States pressure. The same argument seems true of the participation in the 2003 invasion of Iraq, for which the justification appears even more tenuous — there was not even a puppet government in Baghdad to invite our presence, as there was in Saigon. While the government was clearly pressured by the United States, our participation resulted from the government's own assessment of how best to ensure the American alliance. In both cases conservative governments assumed that Australia's security depended more upon a close alliance with the United States than it did upon the specific issues of the wars, and, close as the two countries may have appeared, our government was more influenced by old-fashioned calculations of *realpolitik* than was the United States. Most Australians knew this, and therefore were not particularly outraged by later revelations that there were, in fact, no 'weapons of mass destruction' in Iraq to be destroyed; we joined the 'coalition of the willing' precisely to declare our willingness, whatever justifications Bush and Tony Blair might make.

An apparent willingness by the government to follow United States policies uncritically blends easily with fears of overweening American influence. These sort of fears were rejected by Michael Thawley, Australian ambassador to the United States between 2000–05, who said:

> I have concluded that the efforts of our thinking public class to force us away from the US come from a lack of confidence in the ability of their fellow Australians to manage our relationship with Washington. It is driven by timidity and condescension, not strength or a hardheaded assessment of our national interest.[12]

Thawley has, of course, a clear stake in so arguing, but that does not invalidate his argument.

The most fully argued case of a new dependency is made by my colleague Robert Manne, who rejects the term 'Americanization' in favour of an older one, 'dominionisation', comparing Howard's view of the United States to that of Menzies' for Britain:

> Menzies was thrilled to be welcome in the London of Stanley Baldwin or at Buckingham Palace. John Howard is no less thrilled to be welcome in Washington or at Crawford, George W. Bush's Texan ranch. Menzies and his generation saw in the cultivation of the closest links with the British Empire, economy and culture a vision of Australia's long-term future. Howard has a similar view about the long-term relationship between Australia and the United States ...[13]

Manne's article is worth reading, in part because it makes an original contribution to the discussion of Howard, and in part because it reveals a romantic side to Howard and a vision of the United States as Australia's future that has not been sufficiently explored.

I am to some extent persuaded by Manne's claim that Howard has worked to 'create a new vision of the future: of an Australia deeply integrated — strategically, economically, socially and culturally — into the most formidable empire the world has ever seen', although to make this case he avoids discussing the quite considerable investment Howard has made in pursuing links with countries such as China and Indonesia. In terms of foreign policy it is also possible that the government is concerned to downplay disagreements with the United States, where these do in fact occur, and that its own assessment of matters such as the Kyoto Protocol are more influenced by local concerns (particularly the local coal industry) than by the United States. But I am far less persuaded that, even if Manne's analysis of Howard's views of America is correct, it is likely to be true of Australia in the longer term. As he acknowledges, there is real resistance within Australia (as public opinion surveys reveal) to policies that seem to tie us too closely to the United States. While most Australians appear to support the American alliance, a surprisingly large majority also believe the United States has 'too much power in world affairs' and too much influence on Australia.[14]

This resistance is, of course, partly due to the fact that many Australians believe we are being rapidly embraced into the

American hegemon, and that our sense of national identity is being lost in the process. When I asked a class of about 50 second- and third-year university students at the end of 2005 whether they saw Australia as becoming more like the United States the consensus was largely that, yes, this was an accurate perception. It has become commonplace to point to the ubiquity of American television programs and fast-food chains; one student, tersely if rather cruelly, summed up American influence in the word 'obesity'. To which one might retort that Australian food is clearly differentiating itself from both the working-class British fare we inherited and the equally polyglot self-conscious cuisine of contemporary American 'foodies'. But to many Australians, especially the young and the non-Anglo, the United States represents the only imaginable alternative reality, whether to be emulated or scorned. The journalist James Norman can write scathingly that 'the Howard era has brought us closer to US-style ultra-materialism, where 'retail therapy' is the new buzz word'.[15] Sounds good, but one wonders if Norman has ever walked through the mega shopping malls of middle-class Asia, and does he understand the relentless growth of consumerism in Beijing, Mumbai, and Dubai as no more than importation of an American model?

'They', we believe, are more violent, more ambitious, more patriotic, more fervent. Certainly the statistics would appear to bear out the first claim: one research report claims that the US homicide rate by firearms is *ninety-one* times that of Australia (which has, in turn, somewhat higher rates than Ireland and Japan, though lower than Canada).[16] John Howard's 'buyback' of firearms after the Port Arthur killings of 1996 was widely recognised at the time as going far beyond anything imaginable in the United States, and capital punishment has effectively been abolished here for 30 years, during which time the US has executed thousands of offenders.

If we are becoming the fifty-first state then our politics should reflect this. It is tempting to see in Liberal triumphs under Howard an echo of the Republicans in the United States, rather as Sir Robert Menzies seemed to match Tory dominance in Britain (although his re-election came two years before Churchill's, just as Howard's preceded Bush's). There are some apparent parallels — Peter Costello's espousal of neo-liberal economic management and Tony Abbott's social moralising seem to reflect the two dominant strands within the American right. Howard has clearly attached himself to Bush and his world-view of Iraq and terror, just as Menzies and Holt in earlier periods attached themselves to the American perceptions of the Cold War. Howard himself is a veteran of Cold War politics and assumptions, and his support for the United States was reinforced by the close bonds he and other senior ministers have built with the Bush administration. But not close enough, a cynic may retort, to include sugar in the terms of the Free Trade Agreement.

The Howard government has privatised immigration and employment agencies, moved to a mixed public/private university system, managed to loosen significantly the protections for employees built into what used to be a particularly Australian system of industrial arbitration and wage fixing, and used the Free Trade Agreement to further integrate us into the US economy. Indeed, the Free Trade Agreement marked a major change in Australia's existing commitment to multinational trade negotiations, and seemed to accept major concessions in favour of United States interests. To most on the left these are clear examples of 'Americanization'.

But there are clearly some differences: there remains a liberal conscience in the Coalition parties which has pushed for changes rather different to those associated with the dominant Republican mainstream under President George W. Bush. Thus, on issues such as defending Medicare, or loosening the restrictions on asylum-seekers, and defending the right to abortion, the pressures on Howard come from an electorate, and some sections of his own party, that retains a particular sense of an older social compact that was central to Menzies' vision of the Liberal Party. To date, the language of moral conservatism has been far more muted than in the United States, with some issues, such as support for capital punishment or opposition to the teaching of evolution, confined to fringe opinion even in the conservative parties.

The argument that we are becoming American in both style and content needs to distinguish between the common factors at work in all western societies which are redefining the nature of employment, family structure, and state services, and specific examples of American economic and cultural impacts. As in all western countries, a mix of affluence and insecurity demands a new approach to politics, which leaders like US Democrat Howard Dean and Mark Latham could envision but could not master, and which other than in Britain seems on balance to have favoured conservative parties across the western world. Indeed, our obsession with the United States means we sometimes miss the parallels with other countries: when racial tensions erupted on the beaches of Cronulla in late 2005 this was far more reminiscent of recent events in Europe than of racial tensions within the United States, which are more connected to the legacy of slavery than to the stresses of immigration. Many countries of western Europe have been experiencing the same debates about the role of government and the viability of welfare services which are a product of changing global economic and demographic patterns more than of direct American influence.

It is not difficult to construct possible parallels in our recent histories. The collapse of what Paul Kelly called 'the Australian Settlement', a consensus around social and economic protectionism, resembles the collapse of the New Deal Democratic majority in the United States. Writing in the early 1980s, Kelly saw the five basic ingredients of the settlement as White Australia, industry protection, wage arbitration, state paternalism, and imperial benevolence.[17] All have now essentially disappeared from the centre of Australian public policy, rather as the New Deal's emphasis on the positive role of the state to redress gross inequalities and provide minimum welfare has largely disappeared within the United States. There is a growing emphasis on individualism, reflected in the decline of unions and in support for greater personal freedoms, which could be seen as the result both of larger economic shifts and of specific American influences. The last decade has seen the Coalition successfully appeal to 'cultural' issues in much the same way as has the American right.

Many Australians are fascinated by the United States, but a real understanding of the country is scanty — though far greater, not surprisingly, than is American knowledge of Australia. The massive exposure to American films and television makes for a distorted picture of the United States, so that Australians can feel familiar with the country without acknowledging the differences in the history and ethnic composition of the two societies. While both countries are settler societies, part of the historical movement from Western Europe to conquer and colonise the rest of the world from the sixteenth century on, there remain some significant differences. Both history and geography have dictated the creation of unique societies, even if the superficial similarities seem overwhelming.

The original European settlement of the two countries was predominantly from Britain, but Australia remains far more Anglo-Irish in its ethnic composition than the United States. Even at the end of the eighteenth century, when the American constitution was drafted, there were suggestions of making German an official language, and in the nineteenth century huge immigration from central, southern, and eastern Europe made those of British origin a minority in most American cities. While there is a powerful argument that the basic institutions of the United States retain much of their British origin, those institutions have evolved in the two countries in rather different ways, and the United States is less like Australia than are other English speaking western societies.[18] Indeed, we are more similar to New Zealand, to English-speaking Canada, and even to white South Africa, but Australians are by and large rather uninterested in the parallel colonies.[19] Despite post-war immigration, Australia remains deeply marked by nineteenth-century English and Irish influences. I only realised how Irish were our pubs when I visited Dublin, just as the writer David Malouf had a similar recognition of the familiarity of Scottish mores when he visited Dundee. In recent years there has been more interest in exploring our British roots, in part because of a new confidence born of the reality of 50 years of very diverse immigration. The literary magazine *Meanjin* devoted a whole issue to this question a couple of years ago, unfortunately with an almost entirely Anglo-Australian cast of contributors.[20] As the largest source of migrants continues to be Britain, and British-born residents outnumber those from any other country by a huge margin, British influence continues to be very real.

Most importantly we share a language with Britain and the United States, which for Malouf is central to creating a close relationship.[21] Of course a common language does not, by itself, create harmony, as the examples of Ireland, Iraq, or Bangladesh demonstrate, but it does allow access to other societies. The global dominance of English acts both to isolate Australia and to link us to the wider world; the arrogance of English speakers, who assume that the rest of the world need speak our language, is hardly helpful. The vast majority of images of the outside world reach Australia in American and, less commonly, British accents, so that what facilitates our connection with the larger world also allows us to piggyback on the perceptions and interpretations of the major English-speaking countries. It is common to read columns and articles from British and American writers in our newspapers in a way that would be far less likely without a common language, and it is not always clear if this shows the competence or the laziness of Australian editors.

Australia and the United States share a shameful history of dispossession of the original inhabitants, but Australia is not an empire; our settlement did not involve the sort of warfare the United States engaged in, with Mexico in the 1840s and with Spain in the 1890s, and our twentieth-century colonial activities were restricted to Papua New Guinea at a time when the United States was exerting direct and indirect control in both East Asia and Latin America. Australia did not have to revolt for independence, and thus did not develop the rhetoric of patriotic nationalism so marked in the United States. And Australian settlement did not depend upon slavery, and the racial divide this has left behind. There are real parallels in the dispossession of the original inhabitants of the two countries, but there is no equivalent in Australia to the large African slave population, whose descendants make up about 12 per cent of the United States population. The United States fluctuates in the national attention it pays to racial division, and currently this is a less prominent political issue than it has been in the past, but the ongoing tensions that flow from the central problem of integrating freed slaves into a deeply racist society marks almost every aspect of American life.

It is arguable that contemporary Australia has been more influenced by its Aboriginal and Torres Strait Islander population than has the United States by native Americans, and there are claims that indigenous images, even views of the world, have been appropriated by settler Australia. At times such claims become absurdly romantic, as in Germaine Greer's fantasy of Australia declaring itself an aboriginal and 'hunter-gatherer' country.[22] The red, black, and golden flag of indigenous Australia is certainly a more recognisable symbol in Australia than is any American equivalent, and the concept of reconciliation is officially recognised as a government goal, which is not true of the United States. But if indigenous Australians are more visible than their American counterparts, both groups remain largely marginalised and badly off on almost all measures of socio-economic inequality. Compared to New Zealand, Australia and the United States come off poorly in terms of treatment of their original populations. And the real lesson contemporary Australia might take from its indigenous inhabitants — namely, the need to respect the land and the precarious balance of life in a dry and fragile continent — is constantly mocked by the pressures for growth at any cost.

At one level Australia and the United States share a dominant liberal ideology, summed up in MacPherson's phrase of 'possessive individualism', which stresses both formal democracy and private property.[23] But there is also a distinctive American political ideology, which reflects the ever-present tensions between secular liberalism and Christian doctrines — most significantly, fundamentalist Protestantism, which has marked American history since the first white settlers ('the Puritan fathers') arrived. The nature of settlement and the developing grievances against the British government forced the colonial elites to create a specific American political ideology, in a way that never happened in Australia. Trying to define 'Australian values' in a speech in 2006 Treasurer Peter Costello listed 'values like economic opportunity, security, democracy, personal freedom, the physical environment and strong physical and social infrastructure'.[24] These may well represent conditions we all want, but it is a long way short of the rhetoric of liberty and democracy espoused by Jefferson and Lincoln.

The United States developed a strongly individualistic political culture, with a great distrust of the state, and a corresponding emphasis on rights. The protection provided by the Bill of Rights, although sometimes seeming absurd, as in the arguments that any form of gun control infringes basic liberties, represents an important check on government powers that is less strong in Australia, where conservatives have strongly opposed moves to introduce something similar. One of the consequences of this is that Americans depend more upon the legal system than do most people to resolve issues such as abortion and arguments around school curricula, whether these be prayers in classrooms or the teaching of evolution. In Australia, by contrast, there is an amalgam of common law and quasi-judicial administrative structures, such as the Human Rights and Equal Opportunity Commission and its state equivalents, which are ultimately subordinated to the executive.

Central government, whether in Canberra or (decreasingly)

the state capitals, is more significant in Australia, which has greater expectations and less suspicion of government. In the United States there is far greater emphasis on local control, and city and county governments play a larger role in policing, education, and health services than is true of Australia, where local government is largely subservient to state governments. The union movement has historically been far more central in Australia, and its ability to influence the political agenda produced a very different view of the state, and a particular sense of 'entitlements'. It is fashionable to complain that Australia lacks a sense of identity, but by the end of the nineteenth century the development of the labour movement and associated institutions — specifically the development of the industrial and arbitration system, with its notion of a fair wage for all — provided a particularly Australian vision of the state that was admired by many overseas observers.

Much of this view of the state has been eroded in the past two decades — a matter to which I shall return — but it is retained in assumptions that governments will fund all manner of activities, from public broadcasting to community organisations, which in United States are seen largely as private responsibilities. The state in Australia remains more central and more efficient than in the United States. As Glenn Withers wrote:

Australian public management has ... been highly creative, leading most nations in everything from HECS and Child Support through Immigration Points Selection to controlling

Money Laundering and improving Public Financial Management.[25]

Australians, as the late A.F. Davies liked to say, have a talent for bureaucracy. Americans most certainly do not; one of the striking things about both public and private organisations in the United States is their inefficiency, which is often disguised by sheer wealth.

In part due to its much smaller population, Australia is the more coherent society and seems to have a greater degree of social trust, although empirical evidence is scanty.[26] My assertion is based on many years of moving between the two countries, but is ultimately subjective; I remember many years ago boarding a bus in Berkeley, California, with its customary warning that the driver carried no change, and thinking I would not want to live in a country with so little mutual trust. What one observes in miniature in the United States — being asked for payment before seeing a doctor; having to prepay for petrol or even a cup of coffee; the generally higher level of tension on the streets — seems echoed in such events as the New Orleans floods of 2005, and the crisis of basic civic order they revealed. Australia appears a far more socially cohesive country than the United States, and this is reflected in what Americans see as a slower and friendlier way of life, at least compared to that within their cities.

Australia, too, has a rather different political system, one in which highly disciplined political parties are central. Because of this feature money is less important in political careers, and a wealthy candidate such as Malcolm Turnbull, who entered parliament in 2004 by displacing the sitting Liberal member in possibly the wealthiest electorate in Australia, depended far more on party loyalty than he did on large sums of money. Even so, the dominance of the party machine is producing its own aristocracy in which early contacts and factional loyalty count for more than talent or popularity. In a small way, we have family dynasties, as suggested by the fact that two of Labor's most recent federal leaders, Simon Crean and Kim Beazley, were sons of former cabinet ministers. On the conservative side they are matched by the Anthony family's history in the National Party and the Hodgman dynasty in the Tasmanian Liberals.

Many Australians assert that the United States has a far more diverse press and more robust political debate, despite the constant lament by Americans themselves of the disappearance of dissent. But much of the difference is one of scale: a country of 20 million will inevitably be less diverse than one of almost 300 million. The smallness of scale is reflected in a number of areas, such as Australia's very high concentration of media ownership or the comparative informality of Australian public life. In turn, that difference in scale has a material basis: Australia lacks the rich inland river system of the United States, and other than Canberra has no inland cities that begin to compare with metropolitan centres such as St. Louis, Minneapolis, or Denver.

Australia is not, as the United States has been since World War II, a militarised society. We have a far smaller military establishment and far less employment depends upon military expenditures. Only in a few centres — Darwin and Townsville come to mind — is our civilian population likely to have much contact with the military. Australian participation in World War I is often seen as a formative part of creating national cohesion, despite the bitter domestic debate about conscription which forced two referenda. Certainly the high proportion of Australians who served abroad in the two world wars is significant. But other than during wartime Australia has not experienced the sort of full-scale mobilisation and domestic upheavals that the Civil War meant for the United States in the nineteenth century, nor have the military and violent conflict played such a dominant role in creating a sense of national identity.

Most Australians who write about the spectre of 'Americanization' have an implicit agenda of stressing our uniqueness, whether through claiming a robust national identity or deploring its disappearance. This is a one-way preoccupation: very few Americans lie awake at night fretting about their national distinctiveness. But to invoke 'Americanization' may be the wrong way to frame the question; there are many Americas, some of which have their counterparts in Australian experience, others of which are quite different. It is very easy to imagine a film like *Brokeback Mountain* set in Australia, just as it is impossible to find equivalent misery and alienation on the scale of the huge urban ghettoes of most of America's inner cities. There is always an essentialist danger in comparing nations and political cultures, for, like race and ethnicity, the overlap is often greater than the difference.

As we worry about American values and behaviours supplanting ours the United States itself is changing. Its size and history have made it a more polarised nation than Australia, one in which every extreme of human behaviour seems visible. The apparent triumph of social conservatism since the Reagan victories of the 1980s could well be reversed, as the United States hovers uneasily between attachment to what sociologist Wayne Baker calls 'traditional values' and 'self-expression'.[27] The country can simultaneously contain white extremist militia and feminist separatists, Amish fundamentalists and urban bohemians, and the sheer size of the United States means these groups never meet. Australia, too, has a wide range of cultural and social groups, but with a population one-fourteenth of the United States — the whole country has no more people than southern California — it is far harder for particular communities to remain isolated from each other.

Nor should we exaggerate the differences between the two countries: other than New Zealanders and Canadians, most Americans' lives are more like those of Australians than any other peoples. Yes, they are far more likely to own guns, to serve in the military, to attend church regularly, and to live in 'gated communities'. But Australians are becoming more mobile (the American flight to the sunbelt is matched by the Australian settlement of costal towns such as Tweed Heads and Hervey Bay), and despite their greater religiosity the divorce figures for the two countries are quite close. As our union membership declines, and our public services are increasingly privatised, differences in the political cultures are being eroded, and while the large underclass populations of cities such as Detroit and Philadelphia seem to have no real counterpart in Australia — Redfern is not equivalent to the East Bronx — private wealth co-existing with public squalor is not confined to the United States. An observer from Bangladesh or Bolivia would almost certainly be struck by the similarities rather than the differences between our two countries.

Even so … I have spent almost eight years of my life in the United States, at periods extending back to the 1960s, and I have no doubt that it remains a very different society and polity to Australia. Indeed, the longer I spend in the United States the more foreign it appears, even though there is the constant experience of *déjà vu* that comes from walking round a corner for the first time into a scene that is familiar from television or film. But this is not a uniquely Australian experience, and indeed it brings to mind my first visit to London when I felt I knew the city's geography from schoolboy games of Monopoly.

This is *not* a book about the Australian–American relationship, on which there is already a large literature.[28] But inevitably the relationship will impinge on arguments about 'Americanization', as in Martin Feil's lament that the Free Trade Association could make us 'the Mexico of the Pacific'.[29] Too often issues of foreign policy, economics, and culture are conflated, even though the impact of the US on social and cultural formations is not necessarily the consequence of Australia's close political and military links to the US. One finds complaints about American cultural impact across the world, often in countries which are politically hostile to the United

States. Indeed, the most passionate demonstrators against 'American imperialism' are often users of American technology and wearers of American fashion, rather as leaders such as Malaysia's Dr Mahathir, who constantly attacked western influences, are happy to import western technologies that support their economies.

CHAPTER ONE

Trans-Pacific history

The first British settlement of Australia came within ten years of the loss of the American colonies, and to some extent was dictated by the need to find new outlets to which convicts could be dispatched. Not surprisingly there were links between the new colonies and the United States from early on, as American sealers, whalers, traders, and prospectors found their way across the Pacific. In 1865 the Confederate ship *Shenandoah* arrived in Melbourne after chasing Union ships in the Indian Ocean, and, despite pressure from the American consul, was allowed to refit and sail away. Some Americans took part in the Eureka uprisings, and the famous coach company Cobb and Co. was founded by Americans.

As Australia developed American influences were not unimportant, ranging from the major borrowing of parts of their constitution, such as the basic structures of federalism and the names of the two houses of parliament, to the design for Canberra by American architect Walter Burley Griffin. (The selection of Griffin was influenced by the then minister for home affairs, King O'Malley, who had come to Australia from the United States when he was 30.) A number of prominent

Americans visited the Australian colonies, including Mark Twain and future president Herbert Hoover. By 1908 an Australasian team played the United States in Albert Park, Melbourne, for the Davis Cup in tennis, and over the next 50 years there would be 23 such finals, with the only real challenge for supremacy coming from Britain and France in the inter-war years. Tennis has changed radically in the past two decades, and since 1980 Australia has won the cup only four times.

Nor was Australian influence unknown in the United States, which took both eucalyptus trees and the 'Australian' (secret) ballot from us. As Marilyn Lake has demonstrated there were considerable intellectual links between the elites of all English-language countries by the end of the nineteenth century, connected by a commonality of language, political beliefs, and a sense of racial superiority.[1] Indeed the two countries influenced each other in their development of more and more complex ways of restricting the immigration of 'non-whites'. When 16 American battleships visited Sydney in 1908 at the invitation of Prime Minister Deakin they were hailed as 'the great white fleet', and seen as potential defenders against threats from the Asiatic north. Over the past 200 years more than 100,000 Americans have immigrated to Australia, and have had a significant impact on media, business, and popular culture.

But until World War II, Australia's view of the world was largely filtered though London; it was not until 1940 that we had our own representative in Washington, when R.G. Casey was named Australian minister, and continuous diplomatic representation overseas dates from the end of the war. There were occasional attempts by Australia to define its own foreign policy, as in Prime Minister Billy Hughes's demands for trusteeship over former German New Guinea at the post-World War I peace negotiations, but in general most Australians defined themselves as an extension of Britain, and those Australians who challenged this view tended to be largely isolationist and uninterested in developing an alternative foreign policy. Robert Menzies declared Australia to be at war against Germany in 1939 as a necessary consequence of the declaration of war by the British government.

The attack on Pearl Harbor and the fall of Singapore changed relations with the United States for ever; suddenly Australia looked to the United States, in the words of Prime Minister Curtin, 'free of any pangs as to our traditional links or kinship with the United Kingdom'. During the war General MacArthur established his command of allied troops in Brisbane, and over a million US troops passed through Sydney, their impact reflected in the wartime novel *Come In Spinner* by Dymphna Cusack and Florence James. Succeeding generations of Australians grew up seeing the United States as having saved us from invasion, and this is still invoked as an argument to justify support for American foreign policies — a weak argument, given that the United States entered World War II only after its own territory was attacked.

The signing in 1951 of the ANZUS Pact, and joint operations with the United States in later wars (Korea in the early 1950s, but especially Vietnam in the 1960s and the Gulf and Iraq several decades later) meant that military cooperation with the

United States became central to Australia's engagement with the world. The Menzies government disagreed with the United States on several occasions, notably choosing to back the Anglo/French/Israeli attack on Egypt in 1956 following Egypt's annexation of the Suez Canal. But despite occasional mutters of discontent from Labor's left, all post-war Australian governments have seen the alliance with the United States as crucial to Australian foreign policy. The most strained period was under the Whitlam government, when Australia withdrew its troops from Vietnam ahead of the United States withdrawal, and senior government ministers were loudly critical of the Nixon administration. There were even claims of CIA involvement in Sir John Kerr's decision to sack Whitlam in 1975, and certainly the United States found the Fraser government more amenable.

Throughout the long period of the Cold War, from the late 1940s to the fall of the Berlin Wall and the collapse of the Soviet Union 40 years later, most Australians accepted without much question that we were on the American side in what seemed a cataclysmic division between great powers. In practice, both Labor and Liberal governments cooperated closely with the United States, and Prime Ministers Hawke and Howard made a great deal of their personal relationships with US presidents, even if this was not always reciprocated. In his memoirs President Clinton has two short references to Prime Minister Howard, who receives less attention than the pleasures of visiting the Daintree Rainforest, while Paul Keating, who was prime minister for three years during Clinton's period in office, goes unmentioned, a tacit reminder of the real imbalance in the alliance. Bob Hawke, whose term ended shortly before Clinton took office, is noted for his beer drinking capacity at Oxford.

The Cold War meant Australians increasingly viewed the world through American perceptions, and any independent analysis of Australia's place in the world was discouraged as potentially dangerous, if not treacherous. Australia joined the American system of alliances, signing up to the South East Asian Treaty Organisation (SEATO) a few years after ANZUS, and backing the United States's attempts to prevent the Vietnamese Communists re-unifying that country during the 1970s. The end of the Cold War seemed, for a short time, to allow for a greater divergence from American policies, and the development of a distinctively Australian position in the world, which was enthusiastically endorsed by Keating. Keating did not deny the significance of the United States, but sought to strengthen links between the major Asia/Pacific powers, placing great stress on the Asia Pacific Economic Cooperation Forum (APEC), which grew out of a meeting in Canberra and which since 1994 hosts annual meetings of its leaders, known to most of us for the funny shirts they all wear in the group photograph. For Keating, as for Howard after him, APEC offered the possibilities for expanding trade and security ties simultaneously with the United States and with key Asian countries such as China, Japan, and Indonesia.[2] (India is not a member, but Russia now is.)

The Hawke government sent Australian troops to participate in the United Nations-approved defence of Kuwait in 1990, and there was bipartisan support for sending troops to guarantee the independence of East Timor in 1999, even though American support was initially not certain. During the 1990s Australian participation in peacekeeping operations in Cambodia, Bougainville, Western Sahara, and, most importantly, East Timor were all widely supported, and meant increasing visibility (and funding) for the armed forces. The commander of Australian forces in Timor, Major General Peter Cosgrove, became a national figure and by the end of last century the Australian Defence Forces were the most widely admired branch of government. But even while spending on defence continues to grow, and Australia extends its military involvement into many areas of the world, the defence forces themselves remain relatively small and highly professional, quite unlike the massive armed services, with their very considerable associated economy, of the United States.

The terrorist attacks in the United States in 2001, and the subsequent invasion of Afghanistan and Iraq, restored the American alliance as the centrepiece of Australian foreign policy. A Labor government might have given less enthusiastic support than did Howard, and perhaps followed the lead of New Zealand and Canada, neither of which sent troops to Iraq. But despite strong opposition to the initial involvement in Iraq without specific United Nations authorisation, the majority of Australians appeared to accept that Australia's security depended upon the closest possible ties to the United States, even if this meant dispatching troops to a war whose justification was increasingly murky.

It is likely that the deliberate blurring of distinctions between the terrorism represented by Al-Qaeda and the alleged threat to international security posed by Saddam Hussein, a blurring which was essential to ensure support for the Iraq War for President Bush in the 2004 elections, was assisted by Australia's own sense of threat from international terrorism. For Howard, that sense of shared threat stems in part from his own presence in Washington on 11 September 2001. The Bali bombings of October 2002 which killed over 200 (almost half of them Australian) and which was associated with radical Islamic groups, allowed Howard both to present himself as a national leader and to appeal to a generalised fear of 'terrorists' six months later when the invasion of Iraq commenced. Rather than seeing Australia's role in the invasion of Iraq as a mark of its subservience to the United States it can just as easily be seen as a calculation of self-interest by a conservative government following a century-old practice of Australian governments, which is to engage in foreign wars alongside its more powerful allies as a guarantee of support in a world perceived as potentially hostile.

But fear of terrorism was only one side of the picture of an Australia besieged by hostile forces invoked by Howard. Less than two weeks before the attacks of September 11 a Norwegian tanker, the *Tampa,* took aboard a group of 400 predominantly Afghan asylum-seekers and took them to Christmas Island. The Australian government refused to allow them to land, and denied responsibility for their fate. Eventually Nauru was persuaded, with considerable financial inducements, to allow the refugees to be landed there while the passengers' claims for refugee status were assessed. Ironically, Australia would soon be at war with the very regime the refugees were fleeing. The issue of asylum-seekers became yet more heated in October, when HMAS *Adelaide* encountered a boatload of refugees in the Indian Ocean, and in the resulting confusion it appeared that some refugees threatened to throw their children overboard. This claim was repeated by Howard and his ministers despite evidence from the Navy that it was probably not true.[3] The election campaign of 2001 saw the government parade itself as safeguarding Australian security against the apparently intertwined threats of international terrorism and asylum-seekers, and, in an atmosphere of fear-mongering that recalled the worst days of the Cold War, Howard was triumphant. The two issues reinforced each other; one might wonder whether the hysteria provoked by the *Tampa*, and government claims that 'we decide who comes to this country' would have had as much purchase in a calmer international climate. Already Australian troops were engaged in the attack to overthrow the Taliban government of Afghanistan.

As I write, the political and military alliance with the United States is underpinned by a whole set of ideological structures which aim to reinforce the idea that there is a natural harmony of interests between the two countries. In 1992 the Australian American Leadership Dialogue was founded to promote closer ties, and while it has certainly been a major supporter of most of the current government's policies it has also been strongly supported by Labor figures such as Kim Beazley, Bob Carr, and

Kevin Rudd. When Mark Latham became Labor leader in 2004 he moved quickly to assure Australians, while standing in front of the stars and stripes, that his previous colourful criticisms of the Bush administration did not mean any questioning of the centrality of the alliance. (Latham had referred to Bush as 'the most dangerous and incompetent President in recent history' and the Australian government as 'a conga-line of suck-holes'.) One of the dilemmas for Labor is that the conservative parties, unlike the case in Britain or Canada, were united in supporting American intervention in Vietnam and Iraq, whereas Labor leaders have been forced to balance a wide range of views within the party, and Latham's apology was as much about reassuring Beazley, whom he had narrowly defeated for leadership of the party, as it was about the wider electorate.

There is no doubt, as Robert Manne stresses, that the terrorist attacks on the United States in 2001, and the subsequent armed interventions in Afghanistan and Iraq, have solidified Australia's dependence on the United States. This view is echoed by a number of commentators, including political economist Ann Capling, who argues that the Free Trade Agreement was part of a series of decisions that 'have tied Australia to the American Empire'.[4] While Howard demurred from the term, President Bush has referred to Australia as a 'deputy sheriff' in the region, a reflection that played badly both in Australia and in Asia. Yet, as Howard has stressed, his government has been building relations with key Asian countries with some avidity, and he has matched his own visits to Washington with a number of regional trips.

Prime ministerial visits to Washington, and the constant references to the importance of the American alliance, reflect the growing impact of the United States on all aspects of Australian life, and the increasing investment of American firms in Australia. American investment in Australia exceeds that of all other countries — only Britain comes close. The United States is Australia's second biggest trading partner, exceeded only by Japan, though China is rapidly developing to overtake both. Indeed, the Howard government has courted China assiduously, with far less concern for human rights in that country than has been expressed by the United States administration. Whereas some of Bush's own supporters will raise concerns about China's human rights record, here it seems only the Greens are prepared to countenance any interruption to the courtship of Chinese economic might.

Large numbers of Australians live, work, and study in the United States, and more and more Australian companies recruit senior executives from there; today the two most prominent CEOs of Australian companies, of BHP and Telstra respectively, are American. But all rich economies are increasingly connected by a complex set of financial and trading arrangements, in which the United States is the major national player but by no means omnipotent. Whatever government exists in Australia it will be subject to the fluctuations of world commodity prices and exchange rates, and American influence is often counter-balanced by that of other economies, of stateless multinational corporations, and of international institutions. The frequent reports of international credit-ratings agencies and of the intergovernmental OECD, for example, have an ongoing impact on decisions made by all Australian governments.

Is Australia becoming Americanized?

As already suggested, American influences on Australia date back further than is often acknowledged. In 1914 the first Coles store was opened in Melbourne, based on the model of the 'five and dime store', followed in 1924 by the first Woolworths, which even took its name from the (unrelated) American company.[5] American food producers, such as Heinz and Kellogg, were competing with British and local firms from the 1920s. American films started to become popular after World War I, although their influence was regularly deplored; as one indignant letter writer put it, 'Most of the American pictures shown are absolute rubbish, and an insult to one's intelligence, while the harsh, low-class voices and accent are a continual strain on one's nerves ...'[6] Similar attacks on American cultural influence were found on both left and right, sometimes with very clear racist overtones,[7] but American influence continued to develop. The first Australian Rotary Club was founded in Melbourne in 1921, precursor to a wave of US-style associations and lodges. John Howard grew up in the very Anglo suburb of Earlwood in Sydney, where he attended the Methodist Church, but he also grew up reading the *Saturday Evening Post*.[8] In the 1950s I first came across the *New Yorker* in the Hobart waiting rooms of my ophthalmologist.

Following World War II, Australia, along with the rest of the western world, started to be reshaped by a certain sort of affluence and consumerism that was largely inspired by the United States. Advertising, motor cars, home appliances, supermarkets, motels: all of these were largely imported from the United States and helped re-shape Australian suburban life to resemble the American. In Australia, however, the inner cities never collapsed to the extent that they did in the United States; here, the suburbs begin within a couple of kilometres of the GPO and are neither politically nor culturally separate. The weakness of city government — only in Brisbane does the city council control more than a few square kilometres based on the central business district — has meant that Australia does not make the sharp distinction Americans draw between 'urban' and 'suburban' life. Indeed the 'cappuccino culture' associated with such inner areas as Paddington in Sydney or Fitzroy in Melbourne is spreading into wider areas of the great suburban belts that make up our capital cities, as a new generation moves in and restores pre-World War II bungalows, bringing elements of a café culture with them. Similar families in the United States would be more likely to be found in 'gated communities', deliberately built outside city boundaries.

At the same time the impact of the Cold War, with its associated anti-communist ideology, came to realign Australia as a close ally and in some ways a willing dependent of the United States. As Philip and Roger Bell note, Australia's 'political agenda and discourse changed as it became more integrated into American commerce, military-strategic planning, ideological and political life, popular culture, advertising and consumerism'.[9] Nonetheless it is arguable that the McCarthyism of the early 1950s was not really replicated in Australia, and it was not until this century that the American-derived term 'un-Australian' came into frequent usage. At the height of the McCarthy period a referendum in Australia rejected Menzies's move to outlaw the Communist Party.

Australia is not, of course, unique in its connection to the United States. As two British journalists have written, thinking primarily of the North Atlantic world:

> American culture is so omnipresent that everybody has, as it were, a virtual American buried inside their brain … People around the world feel that they are citizens of the United States in the sense that they are participants in its culture and politics.[10]

Other societies that may seem far different to ours — the Philippines, say, or Argentina — often struggle with remarkably similar fears about the disappearance of their identity into an American-inspired homogeneity. New York and Los Angeles seem as familiar to the average Australian — or Argentinean — as they are to many Americans from Kansas or Tennessee.

Since the 1960s the United States has undoubtedly been the dominant cultural influence on Australia. The counter-culture of the 1960s, and the civil rights and anti-war movements, helped shape the new left of Australia in this period, reflected in the emergence of the social movements of the period. I remember being attacked as an agent of American cultural imperialism for my enthusiasm for American youth culture at the time, and this was probably an accurate assessment. The criticism came from the philosopher Frank Knopfelmacher, who was also a strong defender of the American alliance and our involvement in Vietnam, pointing to the reality that there is often some tension between political and cultural support for the United States. Frank Moorhouse's interconnected short stories of the period, some of which were filmed by Yugoslav director Dusan Makavejev as *The Coca Cola Kid*, record the growing awareness of the United States, even though most young Australians who went abroad still travelled to London, often overland through Asia, rather than across the Pacific. Coca Cola had established itself in Australia just before World War II, and as everywhere else became the ubiquitous symbol of Americanization, summed up in the huge *Coke* sign that used to dominate Sydney's Kings Cross.

During the 1960s the lure of Britain began to decline, particularly for graduate students, who started to look to the prestigious and well-endowed universities of the United States as attractive alternatives to Oxford and Cambridge. Since the 1950s some of Australia's best writers — Sumner Locke Elliot, Shirley Hazzard, Peter Carey — have settled in the United States. From the 1960s on, both the right and left of Australian politics tended to look to the United States for inspiration, as American life became more and more familiar through television and increasing exchange of visits, hastened by the introduction of Jumbo jets on the Pacific route in the early 1970s. The route between Sydney and Los Angeles has now become the single most profitable sector operated by Qantas, which has been far more successful than American-based airlines in attracting business travel. One might also note that the displacement of ships by airplanes as the main means of travel between Australia and the outside world also coincided with the steady rise of Sydney over Melbourne as the country's major city.

The social changes of the 1960s created the period Donald Horne once described as 'the time of hope', and laid the foundations for Whitlam's successful campaign in 1972.[11] It was a time rather like the present, when Australia seemed to be entering a period of unparalleled prosperity, linked, as it is again today, to a resources boom. In a cover story on Australia the previous year, *Time* Magazine wrote:

> The suburbs ... are full of *nouveaux riches* because the country is newly rich. The size of the average car has doubled in ten years; powerboats on trailers choke carports ... Not far away are the supermarkets crowded with housewives in shorts and minis, the fried-chicken drive-ins and the wig-care salons.[12]

The reference to wigs and minis may seem quaintly old-fashioned, but these were people whose support Whitlam won, although many were no more 'traditional' Labor voters than are their children today. Whitlam's apparent failure to manage the economy while in office has haunted the Labor Party ever since.

The US Civil Rights Movement of the 1960s was a direct inspiration for indigenous Australians, and indeed there was a short time in the early 1970s when the rhetoric of 'black power' was borrowed by them. The American notion of 'freedom rides' inspired a group of Aboriginal and white students at the University of Sydney to engage in a similar protest in country New South Wales in 1965.[13] Equally, the re-born American feminist movement had a huge impact on Australia, although no American feminist had the impact of Germaine Greer, who toured Australia a year after the publication of *The Female Eunuch* in 1970 rather in the manner of a rock star. Shrewd observers such as Hester Eisenstein and Anne Summers have pointed to the reality that there were considerably more tangible achievements for gender equality in Australia than in the United States, although visiting Americans often claim that sexism is more pronounced here.[14] American women are more prominent in business and law than their Australian counterparts, but they are less well represented in federal politics; wage disparities remain higher, and bureaucratic institutions directed at supporting women, though less important now than ten years ago, are still stronger in Australia. (The latest OECD figures suggest that while women are paid less than men in both countries, Australian women are less disadvantaged on average than American.) I suspect that Australians have accepted major shifts in how gender is acted out socially more easily than have Americans, even if Americans are more polished in their anti-sexist rhetoric. There is a softer side to Australian men, who seem to feel less need to prove their manhood through violence than in the United States. This is, of course, a subjective assessment, and one modified in both countries by factors of class and race.

In the same way the gay/lesbian movement was influenced by American ideas, but again Australia leapt ahead in concrete gains, while borrowing American terminology. (It is worth remembering that the very popular commercial television series *Number 96* included an openly homosexual character a quarter of a century before American television started making shows like *Melrose Place* — usually for cable.) The criminalisation of homosexual behaviour, a British legacy that still remains in a number of former colonies, was removed in Australia in the 1970s and 1980s, leaving only Tasmania as the exception, and following an appeal to the United Nations Human Rights Committee a federal law was required in 1994 to override the conservative state upper house.[15] In the United States, however, it was not until 2003 that the Supreme Court, reversing an earlier ruling, ensured decriminalisation across the country. This does not mean that Americans have any awareness of Australia's policies, which have been quite innovative in areas such as recognising homosexual relations for immigration purposes. Shortly after the Keating Cabinet decided to remove the ban on homosexuals serving in the military I was rung by a Labor ministerial staffer and asked how we could convey this great news to 'the Americans'. I think he remained unpersuaded by my assurance that 'the Americans' would not be in the least interested.

Australians often fail to recognise the extent to which we have developed our own forms of protest and social movements. Multiculturalism in the United States, for example, has a somewhat different meaning to that in Australia, where it originated as official government policy, aimed at encouraging integration of migrants through provision of services via ethnic communities.[16] And because Australian politics are far less infused with religiosity, moves to recognise gender and sexual equality have created less anger and reaction than in the United States. Yet a sort of cultural cringe persists, and means that Australians — and especially Australian intellectuals — are likely to be more interested in current American intellectual fads than in analysing our own situation. Too many second-rate overseas writers and scholars are lionised in Australia, often at the cost of ignoring our own achievements. The popular equivalent to this is the constant awe of any Australian who 'makes it' in Hollywood, and the slight bemusement that remains when some of our leading actors and directors actually choose to live and work, at least some of the time, in Australia.

As already suggested, 'Americanization' is often a shorthand phrase for globalisation, itself a much contested term. Globalisation, understood as more than another term for free markets and capitalism, is a phenomenon that affects social, cultural, and epistemological understanding, and one that speeds up time and space. Clearly, American images and fashions now reach us much faster than when they relied on ships or even Pan Am clippers. Susan Butler, editor of the *Macquarie Dictionary*, has pointed to a much faster integration of American expressions into our language, and American phrases are now common — 'have a good day' is the most ubiquitous. There is nonetheless a very clear contrast between Australian and American speech, which has more to do with intonation and sentence structure: the rising inflection at the end of so many Australian sentences remains rather different to the more assertive patterns of American English.

New images and concepts come from many sources, even when, as in the case of a television program such as *Big Brother*, we forget its origins were actually Dutch. Some of the business practices and hostility to unions we associate with the United States may owe as much to Japanese pressure. The influences on popular culture are increasingly hybrid and global: films like *Harry Potter* and *Lord of the Rings* are deeply rooted in their British origins; popular music borrows constantly from African rhythms; fashion often originates in Japan and Italy, is universalised through American marketing, and is actually produced in China and Indonesia. Concern about cultural 'Americanization' is widespread, and there is a considerable literature on 'American cultural imperialism', most of which depicts this as a major force in world politics. Americans are more likely to talk about 'soft power' than 'imperialism', but they mean something similar by the term.[17] Australia joined a handful of small countries (Israel, Honduras, Nicaragua, Liberia) in abstaining in October 2005 from the latest international concern expressed through UNESCO's Convention on the Protection of the Diversity of Cultural Expressions, which allows countries to limit the import of films and other cultural products to protect their own, but the debates around the Free Trade Agreement suggested considerable public support for some degree of cultural protectionism.

The language of 'cultural imperialism' often misses the extent to which American products are attractive precisely because they appeal to already widespread values in other societies — or, conversely, because America is seen as an exotic 'other', a place to visit but not to take home. At the same time, to leave everything to the market is to ignore the huge advantages to American publishers and film studios in mobilising resources to control the market. Without some form of government support, as is provided through Australia Council, libraries, and the Film Finance Corporation, it is likely that the supply of local films, books, and television programs able to enter the market in the first place would sadly decline. Funding cuts to the ABC are reflected in low quality quiz and variety shows, whose sets appear increasingly to be put together from leftover furniture in the directors' garages.

For many the extent of Americanization is self-evident, and has already been suggested: American television shows out-rate most local content; American books regularly top the bestseller lists; popular music is dominated by American influence and songs, as it has been for the past century. The Free Trade Agreement with the United States, and proposed relaxation of restrictions on foreign ownership of media, could further increase American influence. A typical comment comes from David Mosler and Bob Catley (who criticise this sort of language when its used by others):

> the tentacles of American cultural imperialism have now extended themselves even in the sporting arena, to Yankee

sports on television, Yank sports in Australia directing Australians away from cricket and Aussie Rules to 'gridiron' baseball, basketball and all of them on television; and the symbols of US college and professional sports everywhere one turns.[18]

They wrote this in 1998, but there is little evidence their fears are justified. Cricket and Australian Rules are thriving, and in both countries the most significant change may be the rise of soccer, which is in fact the most globalised sport, and one where the American influence is trivial.[19]

The traffic of globalisation is more complex than the linear growth in American influence which the language of cultural imperialism suggests. Many young Australians wear clothes and listen to music that seem inspired by Harlem via multinational marketing, but this does not mean they share the views of their counterparts, wearing similar clothes and listening to similar music on similar iPods, in Central Los Angeles, Shinjuku, or Mumbai. Cultures constantly borrow and remake foreign influences in new and unexpected ways, so that Aboriginal hip-hop music blends African–American sounds with older American country music.[20] The 'Lebanese gangs', who have excited so much anxiety in Sydney, are more obviously influenced by Los Angeles street culture than by Islamic extremism, but they are also a product of the particular environment of south-western Sydney. We must always beware of confusing convergence with causality; much of what is changing in both countries is more the product of the inexhaustible inventiveness of capitalist consumption than it is of specifically US influences, and as the economies of East and South Asia become more dominant so too will the fashions they set. Nor should we underestimate the continuing influence of Britain, which is still dominant in many areas of Australian life, whether it be through the institutional links of, say, the Anglican Church or Oxfam, or through the continuing popularity of shows such as *The Bill* or *Absolutely Fabulous*.

I am not persuaded that the large amount of American media available in Australia necessarily undermines a sense of national identity. Australians may watch a show like *Desperate Housewives* in large numbers, but they relate to the characters as fantasy, unlike, say, those of *Kath and Kim*, who have entered the national mythology. One of the oddities of Australia is that the official symbols of the nation are removed from the everyday understanding of what it means to be Australian, rather as the colours worn by our sporting heroes, green and gold, have no parallel to the red, white, and blue of the flag. This does not mean, of course, that there is much desire to change the flag, which is now older than that of most countries. The anthem, despite its clumsy words, *does* seem to have a certain resonance; on the day I wrote this I rode an inner-city train in Melbourne where a busker was applauded after playing the first few lines of *Advance Australia Fair* on a trumpet.

Officially we are defined as a monarchy whose head of state is the hereditary ruler of Britain, but in practice this is meaningless, which is why republicanism has less purchase than it should. Officially, too, Australia Day commemorates the landing of British settlers at Botany Bay, but again it is not seen by most as more than another public holiday. There is no equivalent in Australian mythology to the American tradition of Thanksgiving, or the outpouring of patriotism expressed on the Fourth of July. It is hard to imagine an Australian film called the *Twenty Sixth of January*, although Anzac Day did inspire one of our more significant plays, *The One Day of the Year*. Since 1960, when Alan Seymour wrote that play, Anzac Day has become our de facto national day, a move that was already apparent during the Keating government.

One of the reactions to globalisation is the parallel development of a parochial nationalism, symbolised by the way in which Australian commentary on international sporting events — the Australian Open, say, or the Commonwealth Games — becomes reduced to almost total concentration on the Australian competitors. More complex perhaps, but also a sign of a new nationalist feeling, is the growing interest in Anzac Day and Gallipoli, and the site of the great defeat of 1915 in Turkey has grown as a major tourist destination just as the generation who remember World War I are dying off. Australians seem to me to have a very clear sense of identity, even if it is one that is not always liked by those intellectuals who complain that Australia is still defined by sporting and military success, reflected in the growing reverence for figures such as cricketer Donald Bradman. John Howard understands this appeal; as Judith Brett argues, he has successfully recast the Liberal Party so it appears to represent the nation. He has very skilfully appropriated certain symbols of Australian nationalism

— the flag, the Anzac legend, even 'mateship' — to position the Liberals as the party of the people, and Labor as the party of 'special interests'. Howard himself claims to have 'recovered the orthodox sense of what it means to be Australian'.[21]

Howard's is a narrow nationalism, which shows little interest in the history or cultures of the outside world, not even in the Britain which Robert Menzies seemed to adore. Robert Manne is probably right that Howard is more attracted to the United States than many of us have imagined, but if this is the case it is another sign of his political shrewdness that he speaks for the most part of the American alliance in terms of national interest, not in the romantic imagery which Manne suggests. Certainly the 'Australia' to which Howard appeals is strongly Anglo in its appearance, with little recognition of the millions of Australians who do not feel a particular emotional connection to cricket, the Queen, or the Anzac Tradition. But it would be simplistic to see this as racist, or indeed as purely nostalgic; Howard's vision of Australia may ignore the complexities of our origins, including the indigenous inhabitants and their dispossession, but it has room for those who want to embrace this vision, whatever their ethnicity. As in the United States, the nation is defined as something one can join, rather than something into which one needs to be born.

The jibe of the right that leftists underestimate patriotism and hence fail to recognise the extent to which Australians feel national pride is often correct. I want to avoid the standard laments about the lack of culture, sophistication, and good newspapers in Australia; such laments are often based upon an imagined cultural perfection typically associated with London, Paris, and New York that ignores the extent to which their greater 'culture' is more a product of larger populations and global centrality than of any particular faults of Australia. Our best newspapers stand up very well when compared with those from American cities of comparable size, say Boston or Seattle, and our tabloids are better than those of Britain. It is too easy to make sweeping generalisations without evidence, such as the claim by Julian Cribb that 'One of Australia's charming idiosyncrasies is that it is one of the very few nations on earth where the word "academic" is a term of abuse'.[22] Most countries lionise sports and movie stars, and sport and popular music is the basis for a shared sense of national identity in almost all cultures. The passions aroused by soccer in Italy, Britain, or Brazil are at least the equivalent to that attributed to football in Melbourne.

There are several measures of the popular sense of who is most respected in Australia that contradict the assertions of observers like Cribb. The semi-official position of 'Australian of the Year' has been awarded to a range of people, including scientists, doctors, historians (Manning Clark), and conductors, as well as sportsmen and women. Stamps are an interesting marker of national identity; although they are increasingly produced for revenue from collectors rather than as symbols of the state, they retain a certain degree of authoritative national self-definition.[23] An examination of our stamps not only shows a deep sense of Australian identity, but also an interesting measure of who is recognised as embodying Australian achievement. Australians are more committed to traditional forms of culture — art, music, theatre, books — than is often recognised, and despite the carping — Sweden, and not Australia, has issued a stamp in honour of the Nobel laureate Patrick White — our sense of national achievement goes far beyond the celebration of sports heroes and Hollywood stars than the popular press, like the popular press everywhere, might suggest.

The first Australian stamp issue in 1913 — after Federation the stamps of the six colonies continued in use — showed a kangaroo astride a map of Australia. The map was coloured white, to symbolise Australia's determination to maintain the White Australia Policy.[24] A change of government to the conservatives saw a new series of stamps depicting George V, and images of the monarch remained as the standard design for definitive stamps until the 1970s. It may be worth noting that as early as 1955 Australia produced a stamp honouring 'Australian–American friendship', which managed to combine a representation of the rather phallic US War Memorial in Canberra with an image of the Queen, presumably to reassure Robert Menzies that our basic loyalties remained. Sixteen years later, during the prime ministership of John Gorton, a set of stamps proclaimed links with Asia.

Since 1997 Australia Post has issued an annual set of stamps honouring living 'Australian legends', thus abandoning the convention that other than royalty the subjects of stamps should be safely dead. (Australia remains unique in also issuing an annual stamp for the Queen's birthday.) Three of the issues have depicted sports stars (Donald Bradman, six Olympic gold medal winners, and two tennis players, Rod Laver and Margaret Court). In 2000 the stamps honoured three still-living Anzac veterans. But stamps have also honoured an artist (Arthur Boyd), a popular and a classical singer (Slim Dusty and Joan Sutherland), medical scientists, fashion designers, and, most recently, Barry Humphries, or, in four of the five stamps, his alter-ego Dame Edna Everage, who thus becomes the first cross-dresser to be philatelically acknowledged. A few years ago the National Trust compiled a list of 'living treasures' where again a wide range of achievement was acknowledged.

CHAPTER TWO

The push for unfettered capitalism

T he last decade has seen an explosion of personal wealth and of general affluence, masking the real deprivation that exists in many outer-suburban and provincial and rural areas. The Howard decade might be characterised by the rise of the four-wheel drive and the decline of the public sphere (a widely reported study in 2005 suggested that 4WD drivers were more likely to be intolerant and selfish, especially — surprise, surprise — towards the environment). The fastest growing house type in Australia is now a 'McMansion', with (at least) four bedrooms and a two- to three-car garage, even as family sizes decline.[1] Former working-class suburbs, which seemed vulnerable to Pauline Hanson's attacks on the mantra of globalisation expressed by both major parties, are now affluent in ways unimaginable 20 years ago. The writer John Birmingham describes returning to his home town of Ipswich, once Pauline Hanson's political base, and finding new developments complete with 'a Greg Norman-designed golf course, green belts, artificial lakes, carefully positioned village-style shopping hubs and one gigantic 320 hectare neo-urban meta-concept, the Springfield Town Centre ...'[2] In such surroundings it is not surprising that, as political scientist Don Aitkin argues, we are moving from a society that stresses solidarity to one that privileges individualism.[3]

At some point in the 1980s, following the privatisation of major ventures such as the Commonwealth Bank, more Australians became shareholders than were members of unions. By 2004, over 40 per cent of the adult population held shares directly, and a majority through superannuation funds. In retrospect one might see this as the ultimate victory of capitalism, ensuring that popular support for individual wealth would outweigh considerations of equality and social justice. The growing coverage by media of the stock market — and the way in which rising company profits are always reported as positive, irrespective of the costs to workers, consumers, and the environment — symbolises this shift. When media and casino owner Kerry Packer died at the end of 2005 he was given a state memorial service in honour not of service to the country or for philanthropy, but essentially for being Australia's richest man. Perhaps this should be seen as formalising the triumph of an ethos which could produce headlines such as one I came across in 2005: 'Kim Beazley's alternative tax cuts plan would rob the rich to help poorer Australians.' It becomes ever more important to remind ourselves that taxation is not robbery, but rather a system for providing collectively for services that individuals cannot provide for themselves, and that constantly cutting taxes destroys the shared social infrastructure from which we all benefit.

With New Zealand, Australia saw a radical shift towards a

more individualistic culture and economy in the 1980s, ironically presided over in both cases by Labor governments. On either side of the Tasman, Labor administrations were influenced by a new assertion of neo-liberal ideology across the Anglophone world, expressed by the election of Margaret Thatcher in 1979 and Ronald Reagan in 1980. This would gradually change the policies of all western countries, though nowhere to the extent of the English-speaking world. The new ideology was both a response to and a cause of a restructuring of the world economy, with a collapse of old-style industrial jobs, a growth of new entrepreneurs taking advantage of emerging technologies and rising levels of education which saw most students finishing secondary schooling, and jobs which were once essentially taught through the workplace — such as nursing and journalism — become university subjects. Along with these changes came a set of shifts in public policy, which are radically altering the nature of Australian society.

A consequence of the steady diminishing of the public sphere is a major reconstruction of how most of us see the world, with a shift from a culture of communal responsibility and individual security to an emphasis on individual initiative and a downgrading of the state. A few decades ago one met Australians in their twenties who took jobs in the public service because they were guaranteed life-long employment and a pension; their equivalents today are more likely to be establishing a small business run out of home (possibly their parents' home) with a BlackBerry and a webpage.

The privatisations of the Hawke/Keating period were not

intended to lead to a decline in government services; there was a tenable argument for the government getting out of commercial aviation by selling Qantas, even out of mainstream banking by selling the Commonwealth Bank, and leaving these to survive within the market. (Even so, the experience of the United States might have suggested that the deregulation of civil aviation was likely to have many unforeseen consequences, of which the subsequent collapse of Ansett Airlines in 2001 was the most dramatic.) Nor, unlike Reagan and Thatcher, did Labor under Hawke and Keating seek to reduce the power of the union movement; under Hawke, 'the Accord' was intended specifically to bring union leadership into national economic management, and thus limit the use of strikes and industrial discontent. The government was committed to a 'social wage', recognising that 'living standards were set not just by income but by the full range of benefits governments provided through tax, health insurance, education and welfare'.[4]

But after 1996 the Coalition was able to extend the ethos of privatisation to boost private education, health, and services in areas such as employment and immigration, all of which had traditionally been accepted by both sides of politics as necessary areas for the state to operate. Even Labor state governments have been enthusiastic proponents of 'user-pays' approaches; as I write, Victorian state ministers are justifying cuts to bus services in outer suburbs on the grounds that they aren't profitable, with no apparent recognition of the social obligation to provide transport for the poor, the infirm, and the young. As George Megalogenis wrote, 'Our leaders see the triumph of the open economy as an excuse to privatise society'.[5] Today the most likely political force to remind us that government-run services are not necessarily inferior to those provided by the market are the Nationals. Future generations may be bemused by the assumptions of our era — namely, that all progress is to be measured in terms of company profits and building approvals.

The changes are perhaps most evident in the educational sector, which has become more segmented by class over the past 20 years. Since the Menzies government first initiated state aid for church schools, which at the time was seen as a tactic to take Catholic votes away from Labor, the private sector has exploded; by 2004, over a third of all Australian children were enrolled in private schools, as against perhaps 12 per cent in the US. The proportion of Australian children in private schools is one of the highest in the rich world, and threatens both equality and social cohesion. It is ironic that a government whose rhetoric stresses the need for shared values shows so little commitment to maintaining a public school system, which is probably the single most effective means for teaching a common set of civic values to all citizens. The New South Wales Premier, Morris Iemma, has introduced a 'Respect and Responsibility' program, which seeks to strengthen the teaching of 'Australian values' in all schools, but this begs the question of how far a genuinely diverse society can be fostered when so many children are segregated by religion and wealth. This objection is even stronger in the case of 'home schooling', which allows parents to deny their children any real contact with the wider society, and is gradually increasing in Australia; in 2004 it was estimated there were almost 30,000 students being taught at home, the largest proportion being found, not surprisingly, in Queensland.[6]

At the same time the American model of higher education is replacing one based on the British model, a move that began with Labor minister John Dawkins's abolition of the distinction between universities and colleges, and a corresponding huge leap in enrolments. The current government has taken this shift further, with the acceptance of private universities, the decline of government funding, and, perhaps most pointedly, the introduction of fee-paying undergraduate places, without the sort of financial support provided to students by the best American universities. The government has managed to shift debate on education funding to one of either supporting individual parents (in the case of private schools) or charging individuals for the alleged benefits they receive (in the case of universities), thus ignoring the overall social need for increasing education levels across the system irrespective of people's means. In constant dollar terms, government funding per student has declined roughly by 10 per cent over the past decade, and the amount of this defrayed by HECS payments has almost doubled. But the training of doctors — medical degrees can now cost over $200,000 to complete — benefits society in general, not just individual students. Of course, the traffic is not all one-way; the Labor government's introduction of the HECS scheme, whereby students pay fees through taxation on future income, has been adopted with some modifications in Britain, and Australian universities compete for a share of the very profitable international student market.

Similarly, the Howard government has slowly increased the private share of health care, while recognising the political necessity to retain some form of universal health insurance through Medicare. Any government would struggle to contain health costs, but a Liberal government's solutions lean towards redistributing health care towards the rich in quite striking ways, such as the abolition of a government-supported dental scheme. The American system of health maintenance organisations (HMOs), which link insurance to a set of inter-connected health providers, is beginning to be adopted, ironically by a government which boasts 'freedom of choice'. Given that health care in the United States is generally regarded as the most expensive and least equitable in the industrialised world it is hard to see why any government would see it as a model. But the Free Trade Agreement may well undermine Australia's Pharmaceutical Benefits Scheme, which ensures government support for essential drugs, and is disliked by the major international pharmaceutical companies, including some of the Bush administration's biggest donors.[7]

The greatest success of the right has been to make most people measure their welfare in purely personal terms, forgetting that access to good health care, education, and housing benefit us all. The 'average Australian' suburbanite now sits for hours in traffic jams because of the sum of thousands of individual decisions to drive rather than use public transport, which as a consequence continues to decline; if she is caught with a medical emergency she is likely to wait for hours in hospital facilities that are rarely as comfortable as a roadside pit stop. The mantra of lowering taxes is not even good economics, as a comparative examination of Scandinavian societies reveals. In an interview on his tenth anniversary as prime minister, Howard said, 'I guess working for yourself, working for private enterprise, and not working for the government was something I was brought up to believe in.'[8] Apart from the obvious retort that he has spent most of his adult life on the public payroll, what sort of message does this send to government employees — police, teachers, nurses — who are maintaining the basic services and infrastructure without which society could not function?

What does the new individualism mean for ordinary people? For many it means unparalleled private wealth, and a conspicuous consumption that was not common in earlier Australian history. Read a magazine like *Gourmet Traveller*, with its emphasis on the most expensive meals, the most luxurious spa hotels, and one forgets that several million Australians still live below the poverty line, although means-testing of most welfare measures has at least slowed the growth of the gap between rich and poor. In 1987 Bob Hawke promised that 'no Australian child would live in poverty', but almost 20 years later there are estimates that one in 20 Australian children do, in fact, live in this state. Certainly, unlike the United States, welfare and family-assistance packages have benefited very considerable numbers of lower-income families, and 50 per cent of the federal budget now goes to social welfare and health insurance payments. But soaring corporate salaries have also meant an increasingly affluent upper-class, who are forcing up housing prices to extraordinary levels. Studies suggest a growth of the working poor, whose wages are insufficient to cover basic necessities, worsened by the rise in extra costs for health and education. Like other western societies, changes in housing and family patterns are exiling the poor to outer suburbs and provincial towns, where they impinge less and less on the views of those who shape opinion unless they resort to rioting, as happened in Sydney in Redfern (2004) and Macquarie Fields (2005), in both cases after a police chase which inflamed locals in areas of considerable social and economic disadvantage.

I am writing this in Melbourne, one of the world's great nineteenth-century cities, where the new wealth is literally reshaping the city in a way not seen for a 100 years, with the building of vast apartment and office blocks in reclaimed dock areas, hemmed in by new highways. Yet at the same time the city depends on a public transport system essentially laid out 100 years ago, and some of the community facilities taken for granted then — libraries, good public schools, tram and train lines — are declining. It is only by factoring in such social goods that we can fully measure the claims that most Australians are better off than ever. I am also writing this in a week when several promising students have talked to me about discontinuing their studies because of financial problems. Obviously the affluent society does not provide for the needs of all.

There is some evidence that while the Howard government is regarded as a good economic manager, most Australians are uneasy with the erosion of government services and a sense of the public good. A few years ago the sociologist Michael Pusey spoke with 400 people in groups from the capital cities, and divided his respondents into 'battlers and Hansonites', 'survivors', 'improvers', and 'globalised north shore people', the last phrase revealing the increasing tendency of Sydney-siders to equate themselves with the rest of the country. Across all four groups the majority of his sample did not believe that the economic rationalist policies of the past 20 years have increased individual happiness or social relations. Most of his respondents appeared to have a pretty good understanding of what the 'reform' policies of Hawke, Kennett, and Howard have meant in terms of increasing inequality and declining public services, and to dislike the results.[9] Recent poll data shows that Australia under the current government is seen as richer, but also as less fair, though good economic management and toughness against terror seem to trump these fears. Enough Australians believe that they are personally better off to make the reservations about fairness a difficult issue for the left to mobilise.

For many of its critics the neo-liberalism of contemporary governments seems to represent one face of Americanization. Pusey is quite specific about this:

Middle Australians fear that we are becoming too much like the United States. Indeed, economic reform came to us mainly from Washington. We squander our own strengths by taking the made-in-America model of structural adjustment as a sufficient model for change.[10]

While this may be exaggerated, the dominance of American-style economics, with its neo-theological assumptions of the benefits of the market and mathematical modelling, and of American business schools, has certainly had a major influence upon both private and state sectors in Australia in the past few decades. The decision of Carnegie Mellon University in Pittsburgh to open a branch of its business school in Adelaide, a move welcomed by both the federal and the state (Labor) government, could be seen as symbolising the triumph of American managerialism and economic ideology.

Pusey also points to the influence of American ideas that volunteer organisations should replace government 'as an endlessly self-replenishing font of social proteins'. I have sympathy with Pusey's argument that it is 'mischievous' to regard volunteerism as a substitute for state action.[11] But Australia has its own tradition of voluntary associations, and the strength of groups like the Country Women's Association or surf-lifesaving clubs is an essential part of the social fabric. The evidence suggests that Americans may donate more to voluntary organisations but they do not necessarily have greater active involvement (historically, unions have been stronger in Australia, and church-based groups in the United States). The other response to Pusey's criticism is that volunteerism allows for participation, and the real division is between a right-wing version, which stresses charity, and a leftist model of empowerment. Volunteers are involved in both, but there is a great difference between the rich organising fundraisers for the Red Cross and the disadvantaged being resourced to develop genuine grassroots responses. The numbers of Australians involved in volunteer work is high, and there is some evidence that it has increased over the past decade.[12]

If American influence is a large part of the reason for the apparent triumph of neo-liberal policies, it has been accompanied by domestic growth of the ideological right — the collapse of the Soviet Union was accompanied by a belated triumph of ideological conservatism, reflected in the emergence of right-wing think tanks, in the majority of columnists in the Murdoch newspapers, and in talkback radio, or what Robert O'Sullivan has termed 'outrage radio'.[13] Crucial among the think tanks of the right are the H.R. Nicholls Society, the Institute of Public Affairs, and the Centre for Independent Studies, all supported by mining millionaire Hugh Morgan, whose influence in promoting a right-wing agenda was very important from the early 1980s on. What links all of these, and distinguishes them from more traditional conservatism, is their populist attacks on 'elites', who are defined as leftists, intellectuals, and academics who do not reflect 'real' Australian experience and beliefs. The average Australian does not read publications such as *Quadrant,* originally funded by the Congress for Cultural Freedom, or even the columns in the *Australian,* but they do read and listen to commentators such as the *Herald Sun*'s Andrew Bolt or talkback host Alan Jones, who are aware of the right's intellectual arguments. The advice to leftists that change requires a 'long, slow march through institutions' has been heeded by the right and they have created their own where necessary.

The language of 'elites' has been successfully deployed to attack a range of leftist views as opposed to those of 'ordinary Australians', our equivalent to Nixon's invention of 'middle America'. Carol Johnson quotes Howard in the year of his first election as prime minister as saying:

> You've read the book *The Revolt of the Elites* haven't you? It was written by Christopher Lasch, an American social commentator. His theory is — and I think he's right and I certainly find it here in Australia — that a lot of, for want of a better expression, mainstream people resent the fact that there's a bit of a political elite which includes a lot of people in the press who, in effect, are saying there are certain issues that you, the public, are stupid to be trusted to even talk about. We'll decide it for you and we'll tell you what's good. A lot of Australians feel that issues related to immigration and multiculturalism fall into that category.[14]

The sheer bravura of someone who had been a parliamentarian for 22 years denouncing political elites demands admiration (one Republican idea not taken up by their counterparts in Australia is that of term limits for elected officials), but it also reveals a very clever appropriation of an American analysis to Australian conditions. The apparent divide between a right, who speak in commonsense terms for 'the people' and a left, who represent alien ideas and special interests, has become a staple of commentary about Australian politics, whether it be argued by those who see this as a statement of reality or those who read it as a product of the right's ability to seize the agenda.[15]

One might make a similar comment about Howard's attacks on 'political correctness' and the 'black armband' view of history, by which phrase he apparently means too great an emphasis on the realities of aboriginal dispossession (the phrase was coined by historian Geoffrey Blainey in 1993).[16] In both cases Howard tapped into popular resentments of perceived cultural elites in Australia, and used rhetoric essentially borrowed from American right-wing commentators to make very Australian arguments. The debate on 'political correctness' shows the importance and the limits of imported American rhetoric in Australian political life. Widespread use of the term seems to have begun after a series of articles in the *Australian* in 1991 and was, in particular, frequently used by those on the right to attack Keating's priorities of reconciliation, republicanism, and links with Asia.[17] In one of his early speeches as prime minister, John Howard declared, 'We are not a government beholden to political correctness' but one committed to 'broad community values' and 'practical outcomes'.

Certainly there was an echo here of the language of the American right, and the term 'politically correct' continued to be used as a way of attacking those who seemed too associated with excessive concern for identity politics or discussions of Australian history that stressed the dispossession and death of its indigenous inhabitants. This argument has continued, with considerable and often acrimonious attacks on historians who have written about the underside of white settlement. But even though the debate has sometimes been couched in language imported from the United States, it is a debate that centres on Australian concerns and comes to life where it touches local issues and perceptions. There are parallels to Howard's concerns about the uses of history in the politics of countries such as Japan and Demark, where, as here, American ideas are reshaped to fit local conditions.

One of the oddities of contemporary Australia, where the right now controls the apparatus of the federal government more thoroughly than at any time since Menzies, is the constant attack on 'elitist', 'leftist', 'out of touch' intellectuals who are depicted as somehow threatening society. The editorial pages of the Murdoch papers and much of talkback radio speak constantly of the Fairfax media and the humanities faculties, who seem to loom as a modern equivalent of the Comintern to the terrified forces of the New Right. But then if you only have the government, the United States administration, the tabloid press, and the country's highest rating talk-show hosts behind you, the combined strengths of ABC Radio National and a few departments of cultural studies must seem terrifying indeed. The Coalition's obsession with the ideological left has led to them placing people such as Keith Windschuttle, Ron Brunton, and Janet Albrechtsen on the ABC board for reasons of ideology rather than expertise, and to the former education minister, Brendan Nelson, rejecting grants recommended by the Australian Research Council because he disliked their subject matter.

It is not difficult to see American influence at work here. There is little question that the right has drawn heavily on the far more established and better funded conservative think tanks within the United States, and the enormous power of talkback radio — and such ubiquitous figures as Alan Jones and John Laws seem to draw consciously on American models. The highest rating talkback host in Melbourne, Neil Mitchell, has claimed that 'we [meaning: radio] invented John Howard'.[18] As in other cases, it is difficult to distinguish between indigenous developments and imitative ones, especially as both are fuelled by the same basic needs of consumer capitalism. It might be argued that the media is essentially controlled by the profit motive, and that the rise of conservative ideologues is part of a search for market share, but this would underestimate a quite deliberate attempt by powerful forces within the media and politics to control the agenda. But to acknowledge they have borrowed tactics and language from the United States, as is obvious if one reads, say, Janet Albrechtsen's columns in The *Australian*, does not by itself constitute Americanization.

'Cultural' issues take on a greater significance in all rich counties not only because more people are affluent but also because of the rapid rate of social change, which throws into question areas of life previously 'taken for granted'. But the cultural divide in Australia is not merely a duplication of that in the United States. The 'gender gap', which means women are more likely to vote Democrat than men, is not so much a factor in Australia, although there is some evidence that it may be developing among voters under 30. The growing tendency of non-British immigrants to vote Labor is a result of particular party rhetoric and policies, not a replication of the rather different patterns of ethnic voting in the United States. Church-going affects voting behaviour in both countries, but despite some interesting parallels, it remains a far more private matter, and non-belief is not yet a disqualification for political ambition.

The abolition of the existing industrial relations system, already modified several times over the past decade, will almost certainly mean a decline in the power of unions and a growing disparity in the earning power between those with skills that are in short supply and those without. At the same time, in a flurry of legislative activity at the end of 2005 that reminded one of the halcyon days of the early Whitlam period, the Howard government passed a series of radical legislation, including 'welfare-to-work' measures that seemed to some extent inspired by American models. One of the strongest critics of these measures was a former Liberal minister for family services, Judi Moylan.

The far-reaching changes to industrial relations were born of both local and global (that is, British and American) influences. They reflect the strong conviction of many government figures, not least Howard himself, that the union movement and its ties to the Labor Party are a major impediment to economic growth and conservative political control. Howard is, however, on record several times as saying he believes the American system is unnecessarily harsh and should not be replicated in Australia, although it is impossible to know whether he believes this or is merely acknowledging that this is the popular view. The changes in industrial relations also reflected the influence of multinational companies, particularly the giant mining companies, whose executives were often American (or American trained) and who sought to establish the sort of 'flexible labor market' that exists in the United States — that is, one with lower minimum wages and less protection for workers.[19] It is not surprising that the first real attempt to break away from the model of industrial relations dominant in Australia since the early days of Federation came in the early 1990s in Western Australia, under a state government which was very close to the mining industry. Earlier Labor government interest in 'enterprise bargaining' assumed this would take part within the framework of a centralised arbitration system, which is now being demolished.

These changes were only possible in a society in which appeals to the individual seemed to outweigh any considerations of mutual solidarity or common interests. One might ask whether John Howard, in his stated concerns for the average Australian 'battler' and the traditions of mateship, had ever thought through the ways in which a certain egalitarianism of manners depends upon the guarantees of a decent wage and conditions as 'taken for granted'. The argument that cutting wages will promote employment and economic growth ignores all the evidence, much of it from the United States, that it will also promote alienation and social disruption. As service workers come, in the American manner, to be more and more dependent on tips and casual earnings, their self-esteem is also likely to decline. Henry Lawson's boast that we 'call no biped lord or sir' both reflected and helped frame the underlying assumptions of the industrial system that provided better protection for workers — at least, if male and white — than did most countries. The need to protect (white) workers was claimed in support for the old White Australia Policy; ironically Pacific island countries are currently pushing Australia and New Zealand to admit temporary workers, a move traditionally resisted by the union movement, which has the potential to further depress earnings among the unskilled.

As state services decline we do not have the American tradition of philanthropy to fall back on — this lack is most obvious in the university sector, where the funding of our best institutions is barely equivalent to that of the second tier of United States universities. The generosity of Americans can be overstated: whereas Australians donated 0.7 per cent of gross domestic product in 2004, Americans donated 1.6 per cent.[20] But there is in this country a growing assumption that private philanthropy will increase, and as Australian schools, hospitals, charities, and cultural institutions become more proficient at fundraising there is a real danger that this will become an alibi for cutting back on government services, thus further undermining the recognition that taxation is a system for paying collectively for services that cannot be purchased by the individual, *not*, as some libertarians argue, a form of the state taking what is not rightfully its to take.

CHAPTER THREE

Moral politics and the return of religion

For much of our history, religious allegiances have been a major divide in Australian political life. The Labor splits during World War I over conscription and in the 1950s over the response to Communism involved active partisanship by Catholic clergy, and the Democratic Labor Party — effectively a party of strongly anti-Communist Catholics — kept Labor out of power for 17 years. It is only in the last few decades that Catholics have felt comfortable within the conservative parties, whose leadership until the 1960s was largely Protestant. Here, too, there is a parallel with the United States; the Republican Party, once the bastion of anti-Catholic Protestants, now courts Catholic votes with success, and a Republican president, George W. Bush, has ensured the first-ever Catholic majority on the Supreme Court.

Today there is something of a revival of religion in politics, no longer along the lines of the old division between Protestants and Catholics, but, rather, one led by groups such as the Australian Christian Lobby, that wants to expand the influence of Christianity, broadly defined, on the Australian state. This move reflects the rapid rise of evangelicalism, especially of churches linked to the Pentecostal Assemblies of God, such as Hillsong in Sydney and the Paradise Community Church in Adelaide, home of the Family First Party.[1] A great deal of attention has been given to Peter Costello's and Kim Beazley's support for the Hillsong Church, although a cynic might observe than any politician will happily speak to a crowd of 16,000 at any venue, except perhaps a Mardi Gras Party.[2] It is true that the growth of evangelical and fundamentalist Protestant churches, often in new suburbia, seem to follow an American model — right down to allegations of financial impropriety, such as were levelled at Hillsong in connection with programs directed at indigenous entrepreneurship. As in the United States, the traditional churches are experiencing a consistent decline in attendance while fundamentalist Protestantism is growing, immigration means increasing numbers of Muslims and Hindus, and 'fringe' cults — Scientology, crystals, witchcraft — seem to be flourishing.

There is clearly some rise of religiosity within Australia, but it is not, as yet, on the American scale. Indeed, the United States is unique among rich countries in the extent of church attendance and beliefs in fundamentalist religion. To many observers the rise of religiosity in the United States seems a reaction to the rapidity of changing social mores, in particular the revolution in the expression of sexuality and gender. Richard Florida argues that whereas the first half of the twentieth century saw huge shifts in technology, the second half was marked more by equally large shifts in social arrangements.[3] But there have been equal, if not larger, shifts in social structures in countries like Spain and Ireland, where the hold of the Church has steadily declined with prosperity. Certainly we have experienced such shifts in Australia: when I was a teenager it was considered 'wild' for an unmarried couple to live together; now, de facto couples are recognised, and it is not uncommon for teenagers bring their girl/boyfriends (occasionally of the same gender) home to stay the night. 'I can't imagine how my parents would have reacted', said one friend ruefully, talking of meeting his sixteen-year-old son's girlfriend at breakfast. Far fewer Australians than Americans turn to the churches as a way of responding to rapid social transformations and uncertainties, although Hillsong's appeal does seem to be in part because it provides some sense of community amid rapid change. What is not clear is whether the United States is a harbinger of a far more religious society in future, one in which church-going may become a major factor in determining political attitudes.

The United States has exported its religious sects for several centuries: Mormon missionaries were dispatched to Australia in the middle of the nineteenth century, soon after the founding of the Church, and Christian Science was established in Adelaide at the beginning of the twentieth. In 1958–9 the Reverend Billy Graham held massive revivalist meetings across Australia, without, it seems, much lasting influence on Australian church-going. Australia's history is far more secular than that of the United States, and God is less central to our political language. In her book *God Under Howard* Marion Maddox claims our politics are becoming suffused with religiosity, in part due to

American influence, and gives a range of examples, including the mobilisation of religious parliamentarians through the Lyons Forum (which was founded by conservative members of the Liberals in 1992) and the direct impact of American Evangelical ideas through events such as National Prayer Breakfasts. Direct American fundamentalist interference in our politics, as happened in a number of counties, is harder to establish, although it is possible American money has supported groups such as the Exclusive Brethren, who produced campaign material against Green and Labor candidates in both the 2005 New Zealand and the 2006 Tasmanian elections. I think Maddox over-emphasises the connection to the United States when she speaks of the Howard government 'importing' the policies of the American Christian right — and she herself is careful to stress some differences.[4] Australia has its own weaker history of fundamentalism, connected with the puritanical Baptist and Methodist churches that came from Britain rather than the United States, and that influenced state decisions on matters such as drinking and gambling laws. Perhaps the difference between our two societies is summed up by the fact that the Americans had Prohibition while we had six o'clock closing.

Australia may be in the process of becoming a more religious country, as the charismatic and evangelical churches expand their membership and as more Muslim Australians could be attracted to fundamentalism. But even if the fundamentalist churches grow, they may be less rigid in their positions than their American counterparts, though their ethos is still likely to favour the conservative parties. As David Burchell, one of the first observers to note their potential political significance of the booming Christian churches in western Sydney, wrote:

> Here the Christian ethic of 'Do unto your neighbour…' means doing the right thing by one's actual neighbour, the person next door, rather than by the huddled masses of imagined neighbourhoods beyond. And the injunction not to covet one's neighbour's house and property is understood in terms of mutual respect for property lines and overhanging trees, rather than global humanitarianism.[5]

This insight is very important in explaining why Howard was so successful in mobilising support after *Tampa* against asylum-seekers, who were effectively demonised as being beyond the compassion owed to 'deserving' refugees.

Not all religious influence in politics is necessarily on the right, and some churchmen have been leaders in campaigns against the government's policies on asylum-seekers and industrial relations, where even the doctrinally conservative Anglican Archbishop of Sydney, Peter Jensen, has criticised the government's policies. Indeed, there is a counter-history of churches and politics which stresses the tradition of social justice and compassion, and which argues that believers will naturally find themselves on the left. Conservative clergy like Fred Nile have broken with the Uniting Church because they see it as too socially permissive. Because the dominant tendency of organised religion in the United States in the past few decades has been to support the Republican right, and because church-going is increasingly associated with conservative voting, it becomes easy to assume the right's definition of 'morality' is equivalent to that of all religious groups, although there are many deeply religious people who are socially tolerant and whose religion leads them to stress poverty, inequality, and discrimination as crucial moral issues.

So far, issues such as abortion, gay marriage, and the promotion of sexual abstinence that have been so salient for the Christian right in the United States, and have allowed them to win control of much of the Republican Party, remain largely peripheral to Australian voters, while capable of mobilising small groups. The first sign of an Australian equivalent to the American religious right was Fred Nile's Festival of Light Community Standards Organisation, which was originally more influenced by British Methodism and the campaigns of Mary Whitehouse, although Nile himself had worked for Billy Graham on his second visit to Australia in 1968. Nile founded Call to Australia, later the Christian Democratic Party, which he has represented since 1981 in the NSW Legislative Council. Nile organised visits to Australia of such conservative Britons as Whitehouse and Malcolm Muggeridge in the 1970s, but by the 1990s he was hosting Americans identified as 'anti-militant homosexuals' and 'pro-life campaigners'. Like Family First 20 years later, Nile benefited from preferential voting and the failure of Labor to direct their preferences against right-wing bigots.

The evidence suggests the religious vote is very small, if by that is understood those people for whom 'moral issues', as defined by the religious right, are salient enough to have a major impact on how they vote. Yes, church-goers are more likely to be conservative voters than agnostics or atheists, and the Coalition has benefited from the growing number of voters who send their children to private (almost always religious) schools. There is certainly evidence that the Howard government has been shifting public policy towards a more conservative stance on a number of issues, but it is less clear that this is due to external influences or that 'moral issues' play a major role in how people vote. While some prominent politicians are practising evangelical Christians, the evidence is for gradually liberalising attitudes in Australia around issues such as abortion, homosexuality, and sex education, which have been touchstones for the religious right in the United States. Against the hypothesis that sees social conservatism as a reaction to rapid change, one might posit that rising levels of education and greater contact with overseas social values might lead to the sort of social progressivism sometimes associated with the idea of 'post-materialism'. The evidence is mixed: while opinion polls suggest a liberalisation of views concerning private behaviour, electoral results from the last ten years also suggest an electorate that is primarily concerned with material issues rather than 'values'. But this has probably been consistently true of most elections, with only the occasional example — the Labor victory in 1972 most obviously — where concerns with issues beyond jobs, interest rates, and taxation influenced more than a small number of voters.[6]

Many conservative politicians regard 'moral' issues as central, and increasingly invoke the rhetoric of 'family values' that so inflames American politics. Almost 25 years ago Irene Webley identified the importance of 'the family' (or rather, a particular form of family) to the right:

> The family is the axis of this moral conservatism, [it is] the critical concept that links belief in small government and private enterprise with opposition to abortion, moral permissiveness and humanist influences in education ... The focus on the family ... personalises and privatises social and economic problems thus removing them from the sphere of government action and spending.[7]

This analysis is just as accurate today.

To take an example almost at random, the newly elected Liberal member for Wakefield, in the Adelaide suburbs, gave a long and impassioned speech in the House 'grieving for the modern family', and calling for government intervention to support (heterosexual) marriage.[8] Rather than seeing this as imitating American rhetoric, it is better understood as a response to similar sorts of social changes to those which produced the language of 'family values' in the United States. The irony is that these changes are in part hastened by the very neo-liberal economic and industrial policies espoused by the people who then deplore their consequences. Indeed, they ignore the reality that the 'traditional family', a heterosexual couple with several kids, is declining in numbers as different forms of families and single-person households expand. Government policies work against single parents, even as they become more common.[9]

Howard has flirted with organised religion more than most previous leaders and this has been reflected in some of his appointments, most notably (and disastrously) of Archbishop Peter Hollingsworth as governor-general. When he named Professor Ian Harper to head the new Fair Pay Commission he stressed the appointee's Christian faith, a move presumably intended to forestall criticisms of the new industrial relations regime. Less controversial was the appointment as head of the National Council on Drugs of Salvation Army Major Brian Watters , who came to support some of the 'harm minimisation' policies abhorred by most fundamentalists. In 2005 Watters was replaced by former Liberal minister — and Lyons Forum member — John Herron, who is a prominent Catholic and was ambassador to the Vatican. Despite this, the government has not abandoned 'harm minimisation', although it has been severely criticised by prohibitionist groups such as Drug Free Australia who would prefer the 'unambiguous and effective measures' practised in the United States and are particularly critical of state and territory Labor governments which have decriminalised marijuana use.[10] The United States has indeed pressured Australia to change its drug laws, and when there were suggestions for heroin trials — namely, the provision of heroin under supervision to certified users — the US ambassador intervened and threatened to use his country's power within the International Narcotics Control Board to withdraw Australia's permission to farm poppies for medical opiates.

Several government ministers, most notably Tony Abbott, have supported a socially conservative agenda, although Abbott has at times failed to win support from many in his own party, for example on the prohibition of stem cell research and abortion. Certainly there has been rising concern about the de facto legal status of abortions, with some conservative politicians seeking to restrict it. In early 2006 the fight over whether or not the health minister should have the power to ban the drug RU486 became a surrogate for the abortion debate, with a cross-party coalition of female senators introducing legislation to override the veto of the minister. After very considerable public debate the measure passed both Houses, with strong support from most women and Labor parliamentarians, and with the backing of a number of senior Coalition figures. It is tempting to argue that this marked a clear difference from the United States, where abortion is a far more partisan and emotive issue, and one which has been used effectively by all Republican candidates for the presidency since Reagan.

In the lead-up to the 2004 election, the Howard government introduced legislation to declare marriage as solely between a man and a woman, even though there was no reason to assume at the time that this was likely to be challenged by either courts or state governments. The move was widely seen as an attempt to embarrass the Labor Party by revealing divisions between social conservatives and progressives, but Labor parliamentarians avoided the trap and supported the legislation, while claiming it was unnecessary. It was also almost certainly a deliberate borrowing of American-style 'wedge politics', given that marriage had been a very minor issue even for the gay movement in Australia, although there is evidence that support among lesbians and gay men for marriage rose dramatically *after* parliament voted to oppose it.[11] While the government clearly intended to cause problems for Labor in the inner suburbs of Melbourne and Sydney, where the Greens had some hope of capturing seats, the only electorate where the issue may have influenced a change was in the seat of Adelaide, which swung back to Labor. The defeated Liberal member, Trish Worth, had previously said that Howard's use of the gay marriage issue would cost her the seat. Yet it is worth remembering how fast things have moved: a generation ago almost all Liberal, and most Labor parliamentarians, opposed the decriminalisation of homosexuality.

From the 1980s on Australia was one of the more liberal countries in the world in a number of areas of social policy, such as the decriminalisation of sex work (though under certain conditions which varied from state to state) and the support of drug users through programs such as needle exchange, which were very different from the draconian criminalisation of users that typified the United States. In both cases one could argue that Australia adhered more to a European than an American model, and in some areas, particularly in the national response to HIV and AIDS, Australia was seen as a model by international agencies.[12] While Australia's positions have gradually shifted, most of the basic policies which had slowed down transmission

of HIV — for example needle exchanges — have remained. The
National Strategy against Sexually Transmissible Infections
(2005–8) proclaims:

> Sex education targeting young people should address issues of
> sexual and reproductive health in a holistic and
> developmentally appropriate way. This includes consideration
> being given to the provision of information and support for
> delaying the commencement of sexual activity until it can be
> undertaken in safe and informed circumstances. Education
> should also acknowledge the variety of young peoples'
> circumstances with the intention of building the knowledge,
> skills and strategies they need to respond to HIV/AIDS and
> STIs in the social context in which they live and make
> decisions.

While this is some shift in language from previous strategies,
including that approved by a previous Liberal minister, it is not
the American language of abstinence for all outside marriage.

As in the United States, one must beware of assuming that all
religious organisations are politically conservative; indeed,
some of the most sustained criticism of the current
government's policies on refugees, indigenous rights, and
industrial relations has come from mainstream churches and
senior religious leaders.[13] Even if religiosity becomes more
central to Australian life it will not necessarily follow the same
paths as it has in the United States. Yet as David Marr warned
some years ago, 'ours is a very secular country but the churches

remain the most resilient, most respected and the best-connected lobby in the nation'.[14]

Religion and Multiculturalism

Australia has among the highest percentage of foreign-born inhabitants in the world and, despite continuing high numbers of British and New Zealand immigrants, has seen major shifts in its ethnic and religious composition over the past few decades. The creation of an official policy of multiculturalism, supported successively by the Whitlam, Fraser, and Hawke/Keating governments, seemed to suggest a rather different approach to immigration from that of the United States. Rather than 'a melting pot' in which everyone would be nationalised by allegiance to common values, expressed in patriotic fervour, Australia would support the retention of national and ethnic identities in exchange for acceptance of the dominant political system. Australia, it could be argued, required less of its immigrants than the United States, although in practice both countries accepted that first- and second-generation migrants would retain strong commitments to their native countries. Someone like Melbourne businessman Joe Gutnick could fund the Melbourne Football Club and an Israeli political party, and most Australians accepted the potential clash of loyalties. In practice multiculturalism has meant the funding of traditional cultural activities, often verging on mindless nostalgia for a past that never existed, while the vast majority of immigrants did what most immigrants do and quietly adjusted to the advantages and the problems of their new home.

Australians like to believe that we are spared the worst racist indignities of the United States, but attitudes towards indigenous Australians and those of Middle Eastern descent are often deeply racist, and there is a default assumption among many Anglo-Australians that this is a 'white' country. The patterns of migration have meant that there is no one dominant non-Anglo group, unlike the United States where in many areas of the southwest and metropolitan areas elsewhere Spanish-speakers are dominant, and the question of bilingualism is deeply politicised. Despite small enclaves of migrants in Australian cities there is no challenge to English as the only possible language for any but limited communal activities. Indigenous Australians are usually seen as an uneasy postscript to multiculturalism, being neither immigrants nor part of 'mainstream Australia', and there is considerable confusion around the actual meaning of reconciliation, which remains the official rhetoric regarding indigenous Australians.

Neither the original conception of multiculturalism nor the vicious populism with which the Howard government attacked asylum-seekers owed much to overseas influences, although Canada has a somewhat similar set of policies, complicated by the deep rift between French- and Anglo-Canadians. Because of their history Americans are more likely to define multiculturalism in racial rather than ethnic language, and to associate it with restitution for previous injustices.[15] American census forms require respondents to list their 'race', and require racial origin for a whole set of statistics not regarded as appropriate in Australia, although an exception is often made for those of Aboriginal and Torres Strait Islander descent. While the debate on multiculturalism has become more heated in the past couple of years, as is true of similar debates elsewhere, it is also an area where the major arguments are more likely to be local, and where direct ideological influences from the rest of the world are not particularly evident.

During the Keating period, the philosopher Alan Ryan wrote about SBS television, which is funded to show programs in a range of languages, 'The first person to suggest such a thing in the United States would be clobbered by the defenders of Western Civilisation-as-we-know-it, and find themselves charged with the crime of "cultural fragmentation"'.[16] Since Ryan wrote there has been more concern with 'fragmentation' in Australia, and 'multiculturalism' has become one of the key battlegrounds for social and cultural values, sometimes drawing on American arguments against affirmative action and 'special treatment for minorities', which are largely inapplicable in Australia. Despite this, arguments for an overtly racist immigration policy have largely disappeared, although Howard did suggest back in 1988 that it might be desirable to slow the rate of Asian immigration to preserve social cohesion, thus confusing race with values by assuming that 'Asians' somehow were essentially 'different'. It is hard to imagine him now arguing this way.

Even so, Howard was very conscious of the appeal of Pauline Hanson, who became a national figure in 1996 when her disendorsement by the Liberals ironically allowed her to generate enough support to win a safe Labor House of Representatives seat in Queensland. Hanson appealed to a range of dissatisfactions, but her most widely reported comments were attacks on Aborigines and migrants, and she used her maiden speech to complain that Australia was being 'swamped by Asians'. The evidence suggests that this was a widespread view at the time, and that it has since declined, not because there are fewer Asians but because official rhetoric has shifted (the Coalition understood that Keating's infatuation with Asia was seen by many as code for 'swamping' Australia). More significantly, 'Muslims' have become a new target for anxiety, allowing a certain sort of Asian immigrant — educated, prosperous, English-speaking, and quite likely Christian — to appear very desirable, as in the popular figure of Melbourne's Lord Mayor, John So.[17]

On balance, Australia has incorporated a very considerable and diverse immigrant population with relatively little tension. The 'riots' on Cronulla Beach in Sydney in December 2005, which saw clashes between 'Anglo' and 'Lebanese' Australians, might seem to contradict this, but they were most likely a one-off incident, nasty but not signifying a great deal. Diverse immigration is now a settled part of Australian public policy, and numbers of immigrants and support for immigration have both increased over the past ten years. But there is a renewed questioning of the ideal of multiculturalism, which is seen as code for breaking down 'established' Australian values and social cohesion. As in the United States, attacks on multiculturalism from the right stress a particular version of national identity and history, although the connection with affirmative action and political correctness is less clear in Australia. There is another critique of multiculturalism that could be made from the left, viewing it as a way of maintaining essentialist and restrictive concepts of 'cultural identity' which maintain the established power brokers in immigrant communities, almost always male and often religious, but this is less often expressed.

The recognition that multiculturalism embraces not only diversity but also potential conflicts, especially as 'old-world' antagonisms (Serbs versus Croats, Indians versus Pakistanis, and so forth) are replayed on Australian soil, has recently been articulated in terms of an alleged 'clash of civilisations' between fundamentalist Muslims and the rest of us. Most current concern for social cohesion centres on the extent to which fundamentalist Muslims can be brought into the Australian compact, a legitimate argument that is too easily simplified into attacking 'Arabs', thus ignoring the very large number of Christian Lebanese — and non-Arab Muslims — in Australia. One of the Liberal Party's most traditional conservatives, Peter Coleman, claims that, 'It has now sunk in that some immigrants and their children, many of whom know us well enough, profoundly despise our way of life and even consider themselves at war with it.'[18] Terror attacks overseas and alleged recruitment of potential terrorists in Australia's Muslim communities have created a new fragility in multicultural tolerance over the past few years, and strange alliances have emerged. Social conservatives deplore gender inequality within Islam — several prominent right-wing Liberals have demanded the banning of head-scarves — while fundamentalist Christians, Jews, and Muslims can sometimes agree on the need for protection against 'blasphemy'. 'Our way of life' is itself a constantly changing and contested area; human cultures, like ecospheres, evolve, although on a much more rapid timescale. Any society that is not entirely homogenous needs, for both moral and pragmatic reasons, to provide space for diversity and acceptance of all 'lifestyles' that do not infringe on others.

Successful multiculturalism depends upon a certain degree of secularism which is now under attack from some Christians and some Muslims. (Fundamentalist Jews and Hindus are too small in number and too isolated within their own communities to affect larger debates.) Democratic leaders can, of course, be religious themselves, provided they recognise the line between their own morality and that of the wider society, as was true of both President Kennedy and President Carter, though possibly not of George W. Bush. Liberal democracies are particularly discomforted by groups who argue that respect for tolerance and difference protects even those who would, in practice, abolish both of these attributes. Often a desire to express tolerance makes people unwilling to point to the deep contradictions between upholding common norms and values on the one hand, and allowing for religious freedom on the other.

Some years ago there was a battle around a suburban swimming pool in Brunswick, Melbourne, where the Victorian Equal Opportunity Commission overruled a local Council decision to set aside a period for women-only swimming to allow the pool to be used by Muslim women. This could be viewed either as an expression of cultural sensitivity or as caving in to the worst sort of sexist discrimination, and there is little doubt that attitudes towards gender and sexuality, when justified by religious belief, pose a genuine threat to social cohesion. The Dutch now require immigrants to undergo a test of their tolerance towards groups such as homosexuals, who are arguably more accepted in the Netherlands than anywhere else.

But there are strange double standards at work here, so that politicians will denounce 'bikers' or 'surfers' for their anti-social behaviour, while going to great lengths not to criticise religious groups which practice blatant discrimination and teach hostility to anyone who disagrees with them. In his widely reported speech in February 2006 (already cited), Peter Costello described Australia as a secular state, which 'protects the freedom of all religions for worship'. The other side of secularism, which Costello did not fully discuss, is that the state shall not impose laws based on religious convictions. Costello posited a challenge to this position from adherents of *sharia* law, but gave only one example of anyone advocating this in Australia.

Liberal ambivalence about secularism was revealed in a comment at the same time by Liberal backbencher Danna Vale, who, forced to apologise for a suggestion that allowing abortion would make Australia a majority Islamic country, positioned 'mainstream Australia' against 'Muslim Australians', implicitly suggesting that 'mainstream Australia' is and must remain de facto Christian.[19] In the same way, some Liberal MPs have supported the installation of chaplains in state schools, seemingly oblivious to the Christian bias of the proposal. For the foreseeable future conservative Christians and their political supporters within the government are far more likely to affect public policy than are Muslims, and there is a whole set of legislation and funding which favours religious institutions and, as in the case of schools, allows exemption from equal opportunity laws.

Australia would benefit from a serious debate about the ways in which changing religious beliefs and affiliations might change our political culture. Such a debate would legitimately raise questions of how far deeply held religious beliefs may well threaten the civil rights of people whose behaviour seems immoral to believers. Peter Coleman, who opposed the decriminalisation of homosexuality, might find himself on the same side as many Muslims. But this conversation cannot begin with an assumption that the problem is, in itself, Islam, or that the images of radical Islam in the Middle East have much to do with the reality of Islam in Australia. The publication in 2005 of the infamous Danish cartoons depicting Mohammed had a marginal impact within Australia. Most of the media chose not to republish the cartoons, and there was a small protest outside the Danish consulate in Melbourne. The people who protested may have simplistic notions of what constitutes free speech, but so do the Christians who over the years have picketed films they find offensive, or who pray for rain every Mardi Gras.

Religious beliefs have no more right to be respected than

have any other beliefs, and often they clash with other values: equal status for women, the teaching of evolution and sex education, the right to satirise without censorship. In particular they raise questions as to how far parents have the right to raise their children within a set of beliefs, and what are the countervailing rights of the child and the larger society. Unfortunately, the line between criticisms of religious beliefs, which is akin to criticising political positions, too often shades into attacks on people based on their 'race' and appearance. Nowhere is this clearer than in the current position of Muslims in western countries, who are overwhelmingly from non-European immigrant communities and often face considerable hostility and prejudice. Western societies need to find the means to enforce the basic rules of liberal democratic societies without feeding an irrational and racist attitude which brands everyone who 'looks' Muslim with the worst aspects of fundamentalism.

CHAPTER FOUR

The decline of traditional politics?

I t is a common lament in all western countries that voters are increasingly apathetic, disconnected from political institutions, and likely to support incumbents because of a general lack of interest in the political process itself. As the voluminous debate on concepts like 'social capital' makes clear, it is not necessarily the case that apathy is growing; the claim is rarely supported by conclusive evidence.[1] Younger voters, while not joining the traditional political parties, are often active in a whole range of social movements, some of which, such as the annual 'Clean Up Australia' campaign, seem completely apolitical, and volunteerism is still important in Australian society.[2] While political changes may to some extent be similar across the liberal industrialised world, as politicians respond to similar stresses and complaints, the real life of politics takes place within particular historical and institutional frameworks that are deeply resistant to simply replicating what happens elsewhere. If, as Tolstoy said, every unhappy family is unhappy in its own way, so, too, are polities.

The political system

One important variable is the nature of the political system itself: while Americans fret about the 'imperial presidency', Australians (or, at least, its political junkies) worry about the rise of prime ministerial power. The difference is that we have tightly disciplined parties and no division between executive and legislature — presumably what Peter Costello had in mind in claiming that the weakening of party discipline could bring about an American-style 'balkanisation' of the political process.[3] The quite extraordinary attacks on Queensland National Senator Barnaby Joyce for putting his constituents ahead of his party — the *Australian's* political editor, Dennis Shanahan, referred to his 'six months reign of legislative terror against his Coalition colleagues' — suggests just how strong are the expectations of party discipline in Australia.[4] Interestingly, while party discipline may well have tightened in Australia in the past decade it has become less rigid in Britain, where the Blair government has coped with defectors from its own side on a number of key votes.

Australia and the United States derived their political institutions from the United Kingdom. The Americans, however, based their constitution on an earlier version of the British system, one where monarch and parliament vied for supremacy. By the time the Australian colonies won self-government, the dominance of the House of Commons was established in Britain, and the 'separation of powers' — the lynch-pin of the American constitutional system — had been replaced by a model where the executive depends upon its command of the legislature. This is very different from the American system, where presidents can choose their administration from anywhere, other than from within the legislature. However 'American' our political life may appear it takes place within an institutional setting that is very different, and rests upon very different assumptions about the key relationship between elected representatives and 'the government'. Even when one party controls the presidency and both houses of Congress, as is true for George W. Bush, and was equally so during most Democratic presidencies between 1933–1968, the looser party system allows Congress to act as a far tighter check on the administration than in our much more centralised system.

A key difference between us and the United States is that the conduct of Australian elections is national and non-partisan; there is no equivalent to the Australian Electoral Commission in the United States, where voter registration and the very nature of the ballot paper varies widely, as became clear in the disputed results of the 2000 presidential election in Florida. Neither Australians nor Americans fully appreciate this difference, nor that the partisan drawing of constituency boundaries, essentially vote-rigging by state legislatures, again has no parallel in Australia, although the Legislative Council in Tasmania long resisted any reasonable reapportionment. American elections are almost invariably first past the post, and the proportional system, used in the Senate and the Tasmanian House of Assembly, which fosters the growth of minor parties, is regarded with deep suspicion in the United States.

One of the greatest threats to the Australian political system would be the abolition of compulsory voting, something that at least some members of the Coalition favour. (The government has recently tightened the rules for electoral enrolment, presumably on the assumption that first-time voters are more likely to vote against them.) By requiring an apolitical agency of the state, rather than political parties, to ensure voter registration and turn out, Australia has saved much of the cost of campaigning in other systems, and reduced the possibilities for voter fraud and irregularity. The combination of voluntary voting, local control of the electoral process, and first-past-the-post counting makes for very different outcomes. One consequence of voluntary voting in the United States is that it leads parties to concentrate on mobilising those already predisposed to vote for them, rather than seeking to appeal to those who are genuinely undecided. Compulsory voting almost certainly has the effect of moderating political rhetoric, as politicians seek to appeal to voters with a minimal interest in politics.

While based on the Westminster model, our political system is diverging in significant ways from the British view of parliamentary accountability. Despite huge blunders over immigration matters over several years, the minister, Amanda Vanstone, was not required to resign, just as revelations of ministerial incompetence around the Australian Wheat Board's bribery of the Saddam regime seem, at the time of writing, to have caused remarkably little damage to the government's standing. Little wonder the *Age*'s Shaun Carney could write that, 'Direct responsibility at the ministerial level is almost certainly dead in federal politics.'[5] There was a particular irony in that he wrote this just as the United States Secretary for Homeland Security went on record as accepting responsibility for the mistakes of the Federal Emergency Management Agency in responding to Hurricane Katrina. Party loyalty in Australia is draconian compared to that in Britain, and means a government with a majority in both Houses is basically unchallenged except on very occasional issues.

To conservatives, the move to a republic could be seen as a certain form of 'Americanization', and indeed opponents of a popularly elected president often invoke the United States as a model *not* to be emulated. There is clearly a significant minority of monarchists who reject the idea of a republic because of loyalty to the British connection, and at a less conscious level there may be many who suspect that the continuing myth of monarchy is, in a world of American hegemony, an ironic defence of Australian independence, an argument that is made more explicitly in Canada. Clearly, the symbolism of the Queen, rather like that of the Union Jack on our flag, is understood by the great majority of Australians as in no real sense denying national independence; the common view seems to be that we should change both flag and monarchy, but not just yet.

The most obvious case for Americanization of our politics is in the ways in which pressure-group politics and electioneering appears to be following the US model, with growing emphasis on the power of professional pollsters, political advisers, and lobbyists — of whom there are now 900 accredited in Canberra. Already 30 years ago Australian party officials were paying close attention to American electioneering techniques, and ALP Secretary David Combe considered hiring an established American political consultant for the 1975 campaign.[6] By the 1980s both major parties were closely observing American political techniques.[7] The most recent Australian federal elections saw a heavy emphasis on negative advertising of the sort associated with American campaigns, and a direct influence on both parties of the 'triangulation' strategies of Clinton's advisor Dick Morris — a rather pretentious way of describing the tactics of moving to the centre and declaring independence from both 'extremes'.[8] The Liberals, in particular, have paid close attention to American (in their case, Republican) strategies, reflected in the attacks their advertising mounted against Latham as inexperienced and untrustworthy in the 2004 campaign. But American electioneering is becoming universal; even the pro-Russian party of Ukraine's former president, Viktor Yanukovych, called on American spindoctors to assist his campaign.

Some crucial differences remain. In the United States, individual candidates need to build their own organisation to win the nomination of their party, and are not expected to follow the party line; in Australia, all but a handful of parliamentarians are elected because they have won the endorsement of the party machine. The American primary system, which gives the voters the choice of candidates for their party's nomination, favours those with money, but it also creates a more open political system than the tight control by party offices which is the Australian norm. While Sally Young points to some advertising in party pre-selections, and claims that 'we are headed down the path of American-style big-money politics', the amount of individual money spent in Australian campaigns remains minor, and candidates rely heavily on the party head-office and party leaders.[9] Australian election campaigns are changing, as the older emphasis on formal policy launches and town-hall meetings give way to photo opportunities and constant polling, but these changes have more to do with new means of communication than with external influences.

Lobbyists are less able to influence policy outcomes than they are in the United States system, with its 'iron triangles' of influence linking pressure groups, Congressional committees, and politically appointed bureaucrats; our politicians are less corrupt than their American counterparts mainly because they are not free enough to be worth bribing. Because voting is compulsory, and elections controlled by a non-partisan electoral commission, candidates do not need to spend large sums of money persuading people to register and vote, and public financing, while also present in the United States, helps reduce the cost of elections.

It is sometimes claimed that since the Whitlam government, and the rise of ministerial advisors, our system has become more presidential in style, and certainly prime ministers appear to be far more than the 'first among equals' assumed in some models of cabinet government.[10] This is a tendency in virtually all political systems — maybe Switzerland alone has resisted the rise of the powerful head of government — and it is best understood as a consequence of institutional and political opportunities that allow a leader to constantly centralise control. In the Australian case it requires both parliamentary and party control, and Howard has been particularly skilful in maintaining supremacy within his cabinet, despite very occasional and tentative moves by the Nationals to resist some policies. Howard, too, has jettisoned previous Liberal commitment to state rights, and is as much of a Commonwealth centralist as his Labor predecessors, helped by the fact that, unlike in the United States, the great bulk of state finances is derived from Commonwealth sources.

The biggest changes wrought by the Howard government came as a result of the government's control of the Senate in mid-2005, due in part to Labor's decisions about the flow of preferences which deprived the Greens of one or two extra Senate seats at the end of 2004, and saw Family First's Senator Fielding elected from Victoria despite polling less than two per cent of first-preference votes. (Before the election, few commentators expected the government to win outright control of the Senate, the consequence of their winning four of the six available vacancies in Queensland — an extraordinary result given the system of proportional representation.) Since winning control of the Senate Howard's power as prime minister is perhaps greater than that of any of his predecessors. He has strengthened the power of the executive, and specifically that of the prime minister's office, assisted by threats of terrorism which have allowed him to play a role described by Paul Kelly as 'executive, political and presentational'. Kelly has carefully analysed the ways in which Howard has continued the moves towards strengthening the role of the prime minister, stressing his command of the cabinet, the public service, and the new security apparatus brought into existence since 2001.[11] The establishment of a national security committee of federal cabinet, which includes the most senior ministers plus heads of key departments, security agencies, and the military, follows an American model in handing over key decision-making power to a group in which chief participants are no longer only elected officials but include an equal number of appointed bureaucratic heads. New laws, meant to increase police powers to combat terrorism, have further strengthened executive power to the likely detriment of civil liberties.

Oddly, Kelly ignores the ways in which Howard, despite his stated adherence to the monarchy, has largely replaced the governor-general as the ceremonial face of government, appearing in a constant round of public appearances that could be taken from the Court Circular. It is ironic that Major General Michael Jeffery, the governor-general appointed by a monarchist prime minister, is possibly the least visible occupant of the position since Viscount Dunrossil (1960–1), and even though he is himself a military man he has not supplanted Howard's role in public appearances with Australian troops. Tellingly, Jeffery was not even seated in the front row of the opening of the Commonwealth Games in Melbourne in 2006, although this may just reflect the continuing constitutional problem of where to park the de facto head of state when the de jure head, the Queen, is present.

Influence flows in various directions, and while the Liberals may have learnt a great deal from the Republican successes of the 1990s and 2000s, so too the Howard victories have been influential elsewhere. The Liberal Party's federal director, Lynton Crosby, ran the (unsuccessful) Tory campaign in Britain in 2005, and the Canadian Conservatives looked to his campaigns in the lead-up to their win in 2006. John Howard has chaired the International Democratic Union, an international gathering of 'centre-right' parties founded by Margaret Thatcher, George Bush Sr, and Jacques Chirac in 1983, whose leadership suggests a far wider range of political contacts, especially in Europe and Latin America, than is usually associated with the Australian Liberals. It is part of Howard's cleverness that he rarely speaks of this sort of internationalism, which might appear suspiciously 'elitist' to some of his supporters. But it is revealing that the IDU organises 'a major event' every four years to coincide with the Republican Convention in the United States.

A new Liberal majority?

In the orgy of reflections on the tenth anniversary of the Howard government some argued that Howard was taking Australia in quite new and radical directions, while others claimed that he was merely surfing the changes in socio-economic structures initiated by the Labor governments of

1983–96. Certainly, as is true of any self-professed conservative, Howard appeals to the language of nostalgia, and is careful to present himself as concerned to perpetuate true Australian values. His opposition to republicanism, to an apology to indigenous Australians, and to any statement that Australia is 'part of Asia', were deliberate repudiations of the Keating legacy. John Howard is not an especially imaginative man, and his gut instincts have allowed him to tap a national sense of insecurity that too easily slides into a lazy authoritarianism. But this does not mean he lacks his own vision of Australia's future, and in his way he has been as intent on reshaping Australia as were Whitlam or Keating.

While Howard is far more of a radical economic rationalist than were either Menzies or Fraser, his emphasis is on increasing economic growth rather than reducing governmental power. He does not appear particularly interested in cutting back overall government expenditure, but rather in redirecting where the benefits go; his policies tend to return money to carefully targeted groups of voters rather than aim at improving state services. Unlike American Republicans, the rhetoric is far less about attacking big government, even though economic growth has allowed tax cuts to accompany a redirection of government spending. There has been a deliberate shift to private over public provision of health and educational services, and significant cuts in support for some government institutions, such as the Human Rights and Equal Opportunity Commission, which could be associated with Labor's concern for 'special interests'. Alleged corruption in the Aboriginal and

Torres Strait Islander Commission lead to its abolition in 2005, and its replacement by a National Indigenous Council. While it is hard to argue that ATSIC was a particularly well-functioning body, it was based upon a principle of indigenous self-government which the new structures have abandoned.

Recently Howard removed the Office of the Status of Women from the Prime Minister's Department, where it was first located by Whitlam, to the far less powerful Department of Family and Community Services. Community organisations, which had been well funded since the early 1970s, have seen major reductions in government funding,[12] while restrictions are being quietly attached to funding to prevent community organisations using that funding for advocacy purposes. By 2005, funding for public broadcasting, which means largely the ABC — a constant target of the government for its alleged leftist bias — was the second lowest amount in OECD countries outside the United States.

On balance, Judith Brett may be right in claiming, 'I'm not yet sure they [the Howard government] have fundamentally changed Australia'.[13] Perhaps because she is far less interested in foreign policy, Brett's view is very different to that of Robert Manne, and rather than emphasising the United States connection, she points to Howard's consistent appeals to the symbols of Australian nationalism. She wrote this comment, however, before the government had taken control of the Senate, with the resulting legislation around industrial relations, and she has subsequently acknowledged the fundamental changes this legislation will bring to Australian life. Indeed, in a paper written a year later Brett is more critical of Howard, in particular for his neglect of environmental issues and his lack of interest in planning for the future.[14]

Where Brett is almost certainly right is that most of those who voted for Howard in the four elections between 1996–2005 did not do so because they saw him as an agent of radical change. In fact, he came to office in 1996 precisely by so branding the Keating Labor government. Whatever the practice, his rhetoric has been carefully aimed at reassuring people that a Liberal government would provide security, continuity, and 'trust'. The last word was particularly ironic, coming as it did in the wake of powerful accusations of government lies around the treatment of asylum- seekers in the previous election campaign, but it clearly resonated with those who feared the unpredictability of a change of government. Nor has Howard been nearly as ideological in his choice of colleagues as has George Bush, promoting some Liberals who are clearly 'small "l" liberals' (Julie Bishop, Greg Hunt, Sharman Stone) and equally punishing hard-line conservatives such as Bronwyn Bishop, who was dropped from the ministry after holding several junior portfolios.

Australian elections have been typified by divisions along class lines and a heavy emphasis on economic policies, neither of which are so pronounced in the United States. If, as some have claimed, this is being replaced by a more American-style appeal to cultural issues and symbols this could be seen as yet another sign of Americanization. This debate, inevitably, blurs with one about the electoral success of Howard, and the apparent re-emergence of the Liberals as the natural majority party, if only at the federal level. But there is a surprising degree of continuity in party allegiances and division in Australia that should not be ignored. The next election will be fought between a conservative coalition and the Labor Party, as has been true of all elections since World War I, and minor parties will have far greater impact than in the United States because of preferential voting.

The federal elections of 1998 and 2001 were tight: had a few thousand of votes been cast the other way in 1998, when Labor actually outpolled the government on two-party preferred votes, we would be speculating today on the future of the conservative parties. On the other hand the government polled almost as well in 2004 as they had in their rout of Keating's government in 1996, and there are now relatively few marginal seats which Labor will find easy to win back. During the past decade minor parties have come and gone. The most spectacular example is Pauline Hanson's One Nation Party, but the next Senate election is likely to complete the demise of the Democrats, whose vote collapsed in 2004. The Democrat collapse is largely due to internal party tensions, without which it is possible the Democrats could have been successful in attracting the sort of 'small "l" liberals' who are uneasy with some of Howard's policies. One Nation, too, collapsed in part because of the failure of its leadership to create a genuine party organisation, but it also suffered from Howard's ability to appropriate some of its symbolic language, in particular to reassure voters who felt 'traditional' Australian identity was threatened by rapid social and cultural change.[15]

Although they failed to gain the balance of power in the Senate which most had expected in 2004, the fastest growing political group are the Greens, whose support is strongest in the youngest cohort of voters. It is perfectly conceivable that further losses by Labor, combined with an economic slowdown, could create a new party of the left based on a Green/Labor alliance. Equally, a post-Howard Coalition may splinter from the tensions between Nationals and Liberals, or even between 'wets' and 'drys' within the Liberal Party. The Nationals are most clearly in trouble, with strong independent candidates often able to win away once blue-ribbon seats.

The most common explanation of Howard's success is that he has succeeded in detaching significant numbers of poor and uneducated voters from their 'natural' allegiance to Labor, exploiting the apparent rift between inner-city professional leftists and hardcore working-class unionists within Labor. Yet, outside the over-active imaginations of observers such as David Flint, there is no hard evidence that suggests Liberal voters are less likely to drink lattes and chardonnay than Labor ones, and there is as much of a cultural divide between the established rich areas of Sydney's and Melbourne's eastern suburbs, where Liberal supporters include large numbers of highly educated professionals, and many of the poor rural areas that also vote Liberal. Logically it is the Liberals, not Labor, who should be most vulnerable to division between 'elites' and 'battlers', and it is proof of Howard's political skills that he has been able to employ both terms to his advantage. There is an irony that one of Howard's ministers is Malcolm Turnbull, who, as president of the Australian Republican Movement, epitomised the 'latte- and chardonnay-drinking' elites against whom Howard so successfully mobilised support.

Certainly Howard has been very successful in building a coalition between traditional conservative voters, the elderly, and younger house-buyers in the mortgage belts around the major cities, for whom interest rates and child support are more immediately significant than other issues. Latham sought to counter Howard's appeal to the 'aspirational voter,' who was conceived as hardworking, often self-employed, determined to get ahead, and concerned primarily with immediate family and career. Many of these voters live in the large houses of outer suburban developments. The architect Patrick Kennedy reflected that 'these houses now reflect the same view as our political climate — selfish, conservative and inward looking,'[16] although one might ask whether less selfishness is associated with the more architecturally appealing houses of, say, Vaucluse or Toorak. 'Aspirational' is a slippery term, to say the best, and is now widely used to cover large groups of voters who may in practice have little in common.[17]

Labor frontbencher Lindsay Tanner points to the irony that Labor's best gains in the 2004 election were in safe Liberal seats, where their appeal seemed to be growing among affluent and well-educated voters, while the vote slipped in outer-suburban areas, even those that seemed predominantly working class. Most commentators agreed that the Liberal stress on interest rates was a major factor, and that the government's record of economic management outweighed Latham's talk of tax cuts and of redistribution of funding for schools and health care. (As the Liberals tend to have more sophisticated polling data than Labor, their decision to campaign largely on interest rates suggests this was a major concern for many undecided voters.) The government's success reflected a more long-term transformation of the workforce and the triumph of an individualistic ethos, which is both sociological and ideological. In the past half century the outback has moved from voting Labor to voting conservative, and major mining towns such as Broken Hill, Kalgoorlie, and Mt Isa are represented by non-Labor members. Now many of the outer suburbs whose votes had helped elect Whitlam, Hawke, and Keating are voting Liberal, as mortgage payments become the largest part of household expenditure for many, and Labor flounders to find tactics to change their allegiance.

While protecting low interest rates may well have been the dominant factor for many suburban voters in 2004, they were part of a larger strategy by Howard to depict the Liberals as the party of Australian nationalism, capable of representing virtually the entire population. Howard seemed to borrow American rhetoric in attacking the ALP as the party of 'special interests', but as Brett points out this is an old Liberal theme. She may overstate this, and James Walter suggests that Howard has quite consciously borrowed from 'US market populism' in his attacks on the 'cultural elites', an attack which ironically was also used for a time by Mark Latham.[18] But the attack on the power of unions, which was very much a key part of Howard's industrial relations changes, was as much related to the traditional Liberal agenda as to the influence of American union-bashing.

There is still a correlation between wealth/income and voting, especially in urban areas. Although Labor is increasing its strength in inner urban areas, and maintaining its support among unionists and immigrants, it is struggling to expand much beyond this, and now holds only a handful of seats outside the major metropolitan areas. Bob Birrell has argued persuasively that Labor's blue-collar vote is increasingly an NESB (non-English speaking background) vote, and immigrants, especially from southern Europe and Indochina, are a significant factor in some urban Labor branches.[19] Meanwhile, the Liberals appear to poll particularly well among British migrants, who are concentrated in areas like the outer eastern suburbs of Melbourne and Perth. Howard's appeal to 'the battlers' deploys some of the tactics of American Republicans who, since Nixon, have been successful in appealing to low-income voters precisely by focusing on non-economic issues, and their resentment of 'cultural elites'. Many poor whites have become 'cultural' Republicans, even though Democrats are still more likely to appeal to unionists and city-dwellers — not unlike the pattern of contemporary Australian voting. I have been struck by the number of Labor officials who mention the book *What's the Matter with Kansas?* which seeks to explain the decline of class voting in the United States, and see the argument as directly relevant to Australia.[20]

More than ideology, leadership is crucial, as demonstrated over the past decade in state politics, where Labor has generally governed from the centre against inept conservative opposition. At one level, state politics are largely a non-ideological vicious circle, where oppositions decline and devour themselves until an incumbent government becomes so unpopular it is voted out and the new cycle begins. Yet with odd exceptions, such as the huge landslide to Labor in Queensland in 2001, the faultlines still mirror class and regional differences; at their weakest the Liberals will lose seats to Independents in the northern suburbs of Sydney rather than to Labor. This said, people rarely vote purely out of self-interest, but are influenced, perhaps more than journalists acknowledge, by a sense of what is good for the country, and who can be trusted to provide national leadership. Howard's use of the word 'trust' in 2004 was a canny acknowledgment of this fact, as was the Liberal slogan in the 1996 election, 'For all of us'.

Howard has gradually established himself as a national leader who is seen as able to speak for the nation in ways that go beyond particular economic or cultural divisions. Shortly after his election as prime minister, the mass shooting at Port Arthur led to a move for nation-wide gun control, which showed Howard as willing to offend some of his supporters in what most agreed was the national interest — and one that might be seen as *not* following the lead of the United States. The military support for East Timorese independence in 1999 and the response to the Bali bombings in 2002 allowed Howard to build on his image as directly representing the nation rather than just his party. In his own way, and more skilfully than Keating, John Howard has constructed his own 'big picture' of Australia. It is a picture that combines national pride with a lowered expectation of government, and as long as the economy flourishes it allows the conservative parties to appeal to a very wide section of voters, who in reality may have quite conflicting interests.

For a decade the Liberals have managed an apparent contradiction between 'Howard's role as friend of the Battler and enforcer of global neo-liberalism'.[21] The Liberals, and even more so their National partners, have to appeal both to moral conservatives and to economic libertarians, and the two are far from synonymous. (There are few genuine libertarians in Australia, but there are certainly some people on the right who argue for a flat income tax — clearly of huge benefit to those already well-off — and for considerable reductions in government services and welfare payments.) Tensions between various factions have been severe in most state branches over the past few years, and the Young Liberals, once the source of progressive ideas for the Liberal Party, seem now to be dominated by the moral right, prone to argue for capital punishment and the end of no-fault divorce. Indeed, the ideological influence of the American right is particularly noticeable in the Young Liberals, once regarded as a predominantly social club for the middle-class, which often pushed 'wet' policies on the adult party.

Howard's extraordinary electoral success may disguise the weakness of the Liberal Party at a grassroots level, and the possibility of tensions erupting not only between 'drys' and 'wets' but also between those committed to 'states' rights' and centralists. The tensions within the Coalition, following the assertion by Queensland National Party Senator Barnaby Joyce of the need to represent his constituents, and the defection from Nationals to Liberal of Senator Julian McGauran in 2006, indicates that internal conflicts could create significant stresses on the Coalition. Yet by the middle of 2006 it would be hard to argue that Howard has not established the Liberals as the dominant party at the federal level, able to win more votes than Labor in almost all demographic groups: in 2004, even manual workers were more likely to vote Liberal.

Declining support for Labor leaves it torn between appealing to the immediate demands of 'aspirational' voters and stressing traditions of fairness and better government services. The real challenge is to articulate a clear commitment to principles of fairness and equality as benefiting both the public and the individual. Where Latham tried to do this he was attacked for appealing to the politics of envy (with his 'hit list' of well-funded schools) or for abandoning his own supporters (cutting back on the exploitation of old-growth forests). Nevertheless, his instinct — that there are ways of linking appeals to social justice with the individual experience of many voters — is right. Latham's rhetoric about 'aspirationals' and 'the ladder of opportunity' was influenced by his own electorate of Werriwa in Sydney's outer south-west, once Gough Whitlam's seat, and one that marks the boundary between safe Labor and increasingly safe Liberal suburbia in western Sydney.

Too many in the Labor Party seem to define fairness as centring on greater tax cuts, ignoring the lessons of the 'social wage' and the long-term decline of services that leave us all worse off. Thirty years ago Gough Whitlam convinced Australians that they could demand more from governments, and the lasting support for universal health coverage is testament to his success. In a very different context, Labor today can only win by appealing to a sense of common interest in equality and the sharing of resources, through persuading voters that government matters not only because it taxes and controls, but also because it is our collective means of enriching our lives.

It is not so much policies that Labor needs — outside the press gallery no-one reads opposition policy documents — but rather an over-arching framework that can demonstrate why the government's emphasis on the individual hurts not only most people but also society as a whole. An opposition party must simultaneously hold the government of the day to account and offer an alternative vision that can capture people's imagination. Labor built itself as both a party and a movement, but the rapid growth in affluence and the decline of union membership has turned it into an unhappy organisation of political apparatchiks and union officials, most of whom seem to have lost any real sense of the commitment to a fairer and more egalitarian society that held Labor together in the past. The Labor parliamentary party is more intellectually vigorous than is the government — in the last few years a number of their members, including Lindsay Tanner, Wayne Swan, Carmen Lawrence, and Craig Emerson, have written books on politics — but they are at the same time less successful in convincing most Australians that they have a coherent picture of the sort of society they wish Australia to develop.

Over 25 years ago I wrote a book on Australian politics, *Rehearsals for Change*, in which I argued that cultural transformations were a necessary prerequisite for political change.[22] That message was directed very much at the left, who were then still haunted by the dismissal of the Whitlam government and its rejection at two successive elections. What I did not imagine was that it would be the right who would best learn the lesson, and find ways to incorporate appeals to traditional Australian nationalism into a set of policies that would seem far removed from notions of equality and a fair go. Labor's real challenge is to find an alternative vision of Australia's past and future, one that recognises Howard's skill in reshaping political understandings without trying to imitate his particular mix of neo-liberal economics and social conservatism.

CHAPTER FIVE

How fast is Australia's political culture changing?

Implicit throughout this book are certain assumptions about political culture, by which I mean that set of values, beliefs, and aspirations through which most people in a given 'nation' view politics. Australian political culture grew out of a particular pattern of white settlement, which made for a greater reliance on the state and more emphasis on class solidarity than was true in the United States, and though many of the original institutions this created — from state-owned banks and abattoirs to a very powerful union movement — have largely vanished, it is not merely nostalgia or opportunism that lead Australian politicians to still invoke images of mateship and 'a fair go'. As class becomes less significant as a way of organising one's life, other identities and loyalties increase, and the old tribal party divisions, with working-class Labor ranged against middle-class Liberal, satisfy fewer and fewer people.[1]

Political cultures constantly change, and so they should: a century ago, Australia's political culture rested upon assumptions of white male supremacy and a denial of any indigenous rights that few would defend today. Nor are convergences with other countries surprising, as global economic and cultural influences affect countries in similar ways. All rich societies are now dealing with the impact of greater and more diverse immigration, the competition from rapidly growing economies in Asia, technological changes, and complex security threats such as terrorism, environmental collapse, and new infectious diseases. It is not surprising that there is a growing influence of ideas and images across borders, nor that local responses will often draw upon American voices, which are often the loudest in the room.

Howard has clearly set out to change Australia at least as much as did Keating, even though his rhetoric has been aimed at reassuring Australians that he does not intend to do so. I believe he has made Australia a more conservative country, although it is not always easy to establish exactly what this means, nor how far shifts in the political culture are due to deliberate government action. His government's emphasis on funding private education and its changes to industrial relations are likely to have a long-term effect upon Australia, particularly if they succeed in further weakening the union movement, which can only increase the tensions within the Labor Party. Indeed, one of the reasons for the more pronounced inward and cannibalistic behaviour of the Labor Party stems from the declining numbers of positions available through the union and industrial relations systems, which makes competition by union leaders for parliamentary seats all the more intense. Equally, the growth of full-fee-paying undergraduate courses and the dismantling of student services within universities, under the guise of introducing 'voluntary student unionism', will change the nature of the educational experience for the next generation of tertiary students.

In other areas the government has been less able to impose its will: all its support for stay-at-home mothers will not reverse the economic and social pressures that lead more and more women to remain in the workforce for most of their lives. Australia's need for immigration, which is increasing under the present government, inevitably means continuing decline in the 'Britishness' of Australia, though the change is slower than its opponents suggest. Unlike President Bush, Howard is very skilful at testing the limits of public acceptance, and even among his own supporters it is clear that some of the rhetoric of the ideological right, whether libertarian or religious, is unacceptable. In areas such as treatment of refugees, resistance to the hard line established by Phillip Ruddock as Minister for Immigration — some of which comes from government supporters — has slowly changed government policies.

Most of the change that Howard has imposed grows out of a long-existing Liberal agenda, and owes relatively little to American influence. This is not to deny that the United States has become the dominant foreign influence on our political culture, and provides a de facto model for much of the change currently occurring. The United States has been a presence in Australia from the early days of European settlement, and it is tempting to write a script that sees it as replacing Great Britain as the centrepiece of Australian security, economic, and cultural policies. This script places considerable stress on the Howard government's closeness to Washington, at least since the election of the second Bush administration, and stresses moves such as the Free Trade Agreement and the push from some of its supporters for 'deep integration' with the United States economy.

There is some evidence that most Australians are sceptical of the value of 'deep integration', and, indeed, fears of 'Americanization' are hardly new. From the 1960s on, American political ideas and language have been the dominant external influence in Australia, first through the various movements of the New Left and the counter-culture, then through the re-invigoration of conservatism and the new right. At the beginning of 2006 journalist Miriam Cosic lamented that, 'Just as we've signed on to the American enterprise when it comes to culture, clothing and expeditionary warfare, so have we adopted the terms of its public discourse.'[2] Similar fears were expressed in the 1960s, when Harold Holt's slogan 'All the way with LBJ' seemed to suggest a willingness to become an American satellite. While the unabashed patriotic language of Americans still seems overblown to most Australians, the gap is declining — although it seems odd to suggest that Howard's very effective appeals to Australian nationalism is a mark of Americanization. Our leaders, like theirs, claim ours is the greatest country on earth.

All societies borrow, and borrowings are most effective when they can be merged with existing cultural forms and assumptions. (This is what Philip and Roger Bell had in mind when they named their book on United States's influence on

Australia *Implicated.*) I am reminded of the history of Sydney's Gay and Lesbian Mardi Gras. What originally began as a political commemoration of the Stonewall 'riots' in New York City in 1969, the symbolic beginnings of the modern American gay movement, only became a large-scale event when this connection was broken and the event moved to the Sydney summer.[3] In the same way, Australian environmentalists adopted locally appropriate and innovative strategies, such as the Green Ban movement against urban redevelopment in Sydney in the 1970s which was based on close cooperation with the Builders Labourers Federation, and the Franklin Dam blockade in Tasmania in the 1980s, neither of which owed much to overseas influences. And on the right, the short-lived political support for Pauline Hanson was based on her ability to articulate resentments and frustrations that owed little to the language employed by populist right-wingers in Europe and the United States, even while there were some similarities to the rhetoric of Jean-Marie le Pen and Pat Buchanan.

Peter Conrad may overstate his case when he claims, 'We may share a community of interest, but we have little else in common with America', but he is no more hyperbolic than those who claim we are rapidly becoming a United States satellite.[4] Those who attribute everything they dislike about contemporary developments to the influence of 'Americanization' deny any agency to local actors, which is clearly misleading and reinforces the very processes they are protesting against. There are real limits to how far the current government is able to push Australia towards an American neo-liberal model, even though the attempts to wind back industrial relations suggests a new stage in the attempt. The underlying social contract in Australia is rather different to that in the United States, and the current government is more concerned with the political costs of too directly benefiting the rich than is the Bush administration. In some ways we are becoming less like the United States, even as current rhetoric seems to immerse us further into their picture of the world.

The most important counterbalance to the United States is geography, and growing economic, political, and personal links to Asia. ('Asia' is itself a term of shifting meanings, but to Australians, unlike to many in Europe, it seems to cover everything east of India.) Despite Howard's attacks on Paul Keating's rhetoric of closer links to Asia, he has been assiduous in cultivating economic and political ties with the region. Australian engagement with Asia is of course older than we often remember, and was an inevitable consequence of geography and the end of European colonialism after World War II. Australia had no choice about engaging with the much more populous and potentially powerful countries to our north-west, and strategic and economic interests dictated that this would be the focus of Australian policies. The collapse of the old imperial system of preferential trade following Britain's entry into the European Common Market, and the rapid economic growth of first Japan and then other parts of East and South-East Asia, meant that Australia's prosperity as much as its security became more and more dependent on developments in Asia.

As the global balance of power shifts away from US dominance, as the economies of China and India become significantly larger, and as there develops a greater range of personal ties between Australia and Asia, the period of Americanization may well decline. Despite their attacks on Paul Keating's policies, and some initial clumsiness, Howard and his foreign minister, Alexander Downer, have sought to establish strong ties with neighbouring countries, stressing in particular trade and security ties. The close relationship which Keating established with President Suharto at the end of that leader's authoritarian regime has been recreated to some extent between Howard and the more acceptable President Susilo Bambang Yudhoyono. Indeed, the Howard period has been marked by ongoing deep inter-connection with Indonesia, and despite the very considerable tensions provoked by Australia's role in ensuring the independence of East Timor, the rise of fundamentalism among some Indonesian Muslims, and some Australian support for West Papuan independence, the two governments clearly have a strong commitment to developing close working relations. This is evident from the co-operation between the Australian and Indonesian police in regard to asylum-seekers, terrorism, and drug smuggling. At the time of writing, Howard was widely criticised for 'appeasing' Indonesia by seeking to prevent future asylum-seekers from West Papua.

When we look back on 2005 two events might stand out: the extraordinary outpouring of support for the victims of the tsunami that destroyed parts of Aceh, Thailand, and Sri Lanka on the previous Boxing Day, and a series of trials of young

Australians for drug offences in the region, culminating in huge outrage at the hanging of heroin smuggler Nguyen Tuong Van in Singapore at year's end. Not all agreed; for many Australians the Singapore government showed commendable toughness. But even his critics never saw Van as anything but Australian, a sign of how far migration policies have changed our notion of who is Australian. Both events suggested that there has been a major shift in Australian attitudes: if Australians do not yet think of ourselves as part of Asia, there is an increasing awareness that we have to find ways of deepening relations with the rapidly growing countries of the region. Indeed those two events bookmarked ongoing concern with terrorism in Bali, earthquakes in Kashmir, and swiftly expanding trade with China, all of which are signs of a slow but inexorable move which is distancing us from the Atlantic world. In December Australia became a signatory at the inaugural East Asia summit, a gathering of the major Asian powers that excluded the United States.

Let us reflect for a moment on the way in which Bali has entered the Australian imaginary as a place that is simultaneously distant and exotic and yet as much part of our landscape as many parts of Australia. For several generations of Australians Bali had become the ideal place for a beach holiday, and parts of Kuta Beach seemed as markedly Australian as their equivalents on the Gold Coast where, ironically, much of the business is geared towards Japanese tourists. The bombings of 2002, and a string of arrests of Australians for drug-smuggling in 2005, seemed to disrupt this image, and tourism to Bali has declined, but it remains nonetheless a symbol of Australian ambivalence towards its region — foreign and familiar at the same time.

Much of the contemporary debate about Australia's future is very old-fashioned in that it argues about Australia as if the country existed in a geographic vacuum, rather than seeing Australia as extensively and inextricably enmeshed in an extraordinarily complex range of economic, social, cultural, and political ties with the larger world. We talk a lot of the ways in which constant and changing migration means that the nature of Australia is changing. What we have not yet fully appreciated is how we are also changing as more and more Australians spend some of their lives overseas — as workers, students, soldiers, consultants, and tourists — and how this reflects the larger reality that globalisation is weakening national divisions even as governments seek to expand their control over frontiers.

The greatest problem in political forecasting is the inability to see beyond the immediate to more long-term developments. It may be that the overlapping periods of Howard and Bush mark the high point of certain developments, rather than an ongoing trend. Indeed, if Robert Manne is right, and Howard's support for the United States is 'grounded far less in rational calculation and far more in sentimental dreaming than he or his supporters either understand or would be willing to admit',[5] the likelihood of a future shift in relations is even greater. As cracks open up in the conservative governments in both countries we can start to imagine alternative political futures which may well mean a greater divergence, as well as more significant alternative influences. The growth and importance of China and India will change the environment within which Australia lives, and will inevitably counter the influence of the United States. This is not, of course, unique to Australia; Vancouver, in Canada, has a far larger Asian-born population than any major Australian city. But even in an age of large jets and electronic communication, Australia's geographic position is still important, and growing ties with Asia are important in ways not true for other predominantly European countries. What happens in Jakarta or Manila has a direct impact in Australia, far greater than the impact in North America or Europe.

For many Australians the United States remains the ultimate insurance policy against aggression, even though a significant number of Australians would argue that it is our very closeness to United States policy that makes us an attractive target for attack. When Bob Carr interviewed the American author Gore Vidal for the ABC in January 2006, Carr explicitly argued that the alliance saved Australia very considerable investment in its own defence, a proposition that should be contested: the intervention in Iraq is likely to end up far more costly in terms of Australia's relations with the Islamic world, including very important countries in our immediate region, than is gained by any short-term friendship from the current US administration. When Americans think of Australia, which is not often, they see it as the perfect ally: one commentator on the decline of support for the United States pointed to falling support for American foreign policies in Australia as the ultimate test of American failure.[6] But the reality is that the United States will defend

Australia's interests if it believes them to be consistent with its own, and this is so whether or not our governments constantly proclaim their support for the United States.

The current government shows some enthusiasm for satrapy status, an enthusiasm that seems increasingly unattractive as President Bush's domestic popularity continues to fall due to the worsening situation in Iraq. In all probability a future Australian government will need to distance itself from the enthusiasm of this one for the United States alliance, an enthusiasm which at times has resembled a schoolboy crush rather than a carefully thought-through foreign policy. But any government in the foreseeable future will need to manage a relationship that is obviously far more important to us than it can ever be to them.

For some Australians the United States represents the future, the best, the most advanced, and therefore a model to be emulated. One meets such Australians sometimes among graduates from American business schools, impatient with what they see as the nostalgic provincialism of Australian life. One can also meet Australians who can only talk about the United States as the embodiment of all they dislike, though there is both a conservative and a radical version of this, which comes together in agreement that we must remain vigilant against encroaching Americanization. Not surprisingly, most of us fall somewhere in between, and the predominant mood is probably one of ambivalence. When Hurricane Katrina destroyed New Orleans in late 2005 most Australians were shocked by the images of poverty, inequality, and violence that were revealed in the constant images from the United States. Even those Australians who were enthusiastically pro-American in foreign policy agreed there were domestic problems and inequalities in the United States we would not wish to emulate.

At the same time, many on the left find much to admire in the United States. During the 1960s Jim Cairns, leader of the Labor left, visited the United States and remarked on the extent and vigour of dissent. Thirty years later Don Watson lamented:

> Would that we had the Americans' confidence. A small portion of their inventiveness. Just one of their best universities or research institutes. Two of their best five hundred companies. Some of their instinct for philanthropy. Some of their genius … Would that we had been so open and so civilised.[7]

(But a few pages later, in a glorious piece of inconsistency, he complains that Americans 'missed a stage in the progress of western civilisation'.) This comment is echoed in the fear expressed by political scientist Ian Marsh that the neo-liberal consensus of the major parties might 'move the forms and patterns of Australian civic life in the direction of the United States, without the idealism that also tempers American politics'.[8] For all the emphasis on right-wing appropriation of American ideas, the Australian left also finds inspiration in American opponents of the status quo such as Noam Chomsky or Barbara Ehrenreich. Not only did Labor women borrow the idea of setting up a fundraising group for women candidates, they even took over the American name, Emily's List.

To Watson's list I would add the commitment to civil liberties and individual rights that makes so many Americans willing to defy authority. There is something shameful in Australians' acquiescence in this government's disregard for civil liberties, whether it be those of asylum-seekers or of alleged terrorist sympathisers like David Hicks, who has been held in Guantanamo Bay for over four years without proper trial or the minimum protection the British government offered its citizens in similar circumstances. The occasional debate about the need for an Australian Bill of Rights would benefit from an infusion of American-style commitment.

The constant fear lurking behind much current leftist thinking — namely, that we are being swallowed by the hegemony of the United States — is misguided. The basic cultural differences between the two countries, which writers such as Watson acknowledge, are not easily shaken by US culture — indeed, globalisation runs in many unexpected directions, and even as we import American basketball and fast foods so too we are constantly remaking our sense of what it is to be Australian in ways which keep us clearly distinct. Yes, globalisation means that much of what was traditionally valued is being lost, and this is not necessarily a sign of progress. It is not hard to find examples where we look more and more like the United States. Our outer suburbs, with their multi-car garaged McMansions and their huge shopping malls, seem already like slices of American suburbia, but so too does today's stress on individual achievement and ostentatious wealth. When Packer's biographer is quoted as saying, 'In this country to be aggressive and successful and fight for what you want and tread on anyone in the way is somehow admired', it is hard not to believe he is talking of the United States.[9]

In the end, the ways in which we manage and imagine the impact of globalisation is our collective choice, arrived at through domestic political debates and campaigns. The United States is not responsible for the election of the Howard government, nor indeed for the weaknesses of its opponents. We cannot blame Americans for the parochialism that means our eyes remain rigidly fixed on the English-speaking countries of the North Atlantic. Australians remain oddly indifferent to the experience of other middle-rank countries which might offer us more interesting models than either the United States or the economic giants of East Asia: how many Australians show much interest in, say, Brazil, Canada, or the Netherlands? Yet these are all countries whose social and cultural policies offer interesting alternatives to those which come from Washington and London. Australia's geographic position, its diverse ethnic background, and its relations with 50 other states through the Commonwealth of Nations all offer real possibilities of far more complex relations with the world than one determined through American eyes. Interest in a wider range of countries might save Australia from some of the worst consequences of its North-Atlantic cringe, whether expressed through an over-enthusiastic embrace of Thatcherism in the 1980s or of George W. Bush in the 2000s.

Precisely because we do not belong to any obvious regional grouping, Australia has an interest in building relations with middle-sized states across the world, and in fostering a range of multilateral institutions which the current government has been, by and large, de-emphasising. (It also has an interest in a more generous approach to global redistribution of wealth, where Australia's record of foreign assistance is one of the poorer among rich countries.) Expanding relations with a much wider range of countries can, in turn, promote a more vigorous and challenging search for ways to re-imagine Australia. At the beginning of this book I compared the French response to changes in industrial conditions to ours. It is fashionable to attack France as a stagnant economy with growing social divisions. Yet, a more balanced appreciation might suggest that the French have found a more attractive balance between state and citizen than that in the English-speaking societies. There is a danger that we all, left and right alike, become too fixated on the United States, and accept their own evaluation that they are the centre of all that matters. The lure of New York and Los Angeles is a powerful one in a world where they symbolise raw wealth and power, and it is a lure felt by many right across the political spectrum. The United States has much to teach us, but too often it seems to be the only model, leading us to forget the full range of available economic, political, and cultural options.

Australia's future need not be a nationalist one. Indeed, our very cynicism about the trappings of nationalism might make Australians more able to adapt to an internationalist world. Howard's rhetoric is certainly hostile to cosmopolitanism and the creation of global norms, but this hostility is far more shallow in Australia than it is in the United States. If the new story we want to build for ourselves can encompass the world rather than just the nation, our dreamings will be more important and a better antidote to the influence of 'Americanization' than a vision which remains solely centred on definitions of the 'nation'.

Notes

Introduction

1. Brian Courtis, 'Now, that wasn't so bad', *Sunday Age,* 19 June 2005
2. Jim Davidson, 'De-dominionisation revisited', *AJPH* 51/1, March 2005, p. 12
3. John Birmingham, *A Time for War,* Quarterly Essay 20, Black Inc, 2005, p. 57
4. See for example, Brendon O'Connor & Martin Griffiths, *The Rise of anti-Americanism,* Routledge, NY, 2005
5. Quoted by Ray Aitchison, *The Americans in Australia,* Australian Educational Press, Blackburn, 1986, p. 51
6. See David Mosler & Bob Catley, *America and Americans in Australia,* Praeger, Westport, 1998, pp. 8-9
7. Don Watson, *Rabbit Syndrome,* Quarterly Essay 4, Black Inc, 2001, p. 42
8. Wayne Swan, *Postcode: the splintering of a nation,* Pluto, Sydney 2005, p. 22
9. Peter Beilharz, 'Australia: the Unhappy Country, or, A Tale of Two Nations', *Thesis Eleven* 82, 2005, p. 84
10. David Williamson, 'Cruise Ship Australia', *The Bulletin,* 10 October, 2005
11. Michael Sexton, *War for the Asking,* Penguin, 1981; Richard Leaver, 'Patterns of Dependence in post-war Australian Foreign Policy' in Leaver & Cox, *Middling, Meddling, Muddling: Issues in Australian Foreign Policy,* Allen & Unwin, 1997
12. Michael Thawley, 'Why Uncle Sam is still good for us', *The Age,* 9 November 2005
13. Robert Manne, 'Little America', *The Monthly,* March 2006, p. 32
14. Murray Goot, 'Neither entirely comfortable nor wholly relaxed: public opinion, electoral politics and foreign policy' in Cotton & Ravenhill, *Trading on Alliance Security: Australia in World Affairs 2001–5,* Oxford University Press, Melbourne, 2006
15. James Norman, 'Howard's young people are shallow and disengaged', *The Age,* 23 February 2006
16. Johns Hopkins Center for Gun Policy and Research cited by Garry Wills, 'Jimmy Carter and the Culture of Death', *New York Review of Books,* 9 February 2006

17. Paul Kelly, *The End of Certainty,* Allen & Unwin, 1992, pp. 1–2

18. On comparisons between 'settler societies' see S. M. Lipset, *American exceptionalism : a double-edged sword,* Norton, NY, 1996

19. See Jim Davidson, 'Dominion Culture', *Meanjin* 68/3, 2004, pp. 75–84

20. *British…ish Meanjin,* 63/3, 2004

21. David Malouf, *Made in England: Australia's British Inheritance,* Quarterly Essay 12, Black Inc, 2003

22. Germaine Greer, *Whitefella Jump Up,* Quarterly Essay 11, Black Inc, 2003

23. C.B. Macpherson, *The political theory of possessive individualism: Hobbes to Locke,* OUP, 1962

24. Peter Costello, 'Worth promoting, worth defending: Australian citizenship, what it means and how to nurture it', address to the Sydney Institute, 23 February 2006

25. Glenn Withers review of John Braithwaite, *Markets in Vice; Markets in Virtue* in *Dialogue,* Canberra Academy of the Social Sciences 24/3, 2005, pp. 81–2

26. See Clive Bean, 'Is there a crisis of trust in Australia?' in Wilson et.al., *Australian Social Attitudes,* UNSW Press, 2005, pp. 122-40

27. Wayne Baker, *America's Crisis of Values,* Princeton University Press, 2005

28. See for example: Bruce Grant, *Fatal Attraction,* Black Inc, 2004; John Langmore, *Dealing with America,* UNSW Press, 2005

29. Martin Feil, 'Australia's left holding trade's billion dollar baby', *The Age,* 10 January 2006

30. Paul Barry quoted by Tim Elliott, 'Under the skin', *Sunday Life, Sunday Age,* 5 March 2006, p. 23

Chapter 1

1. Marilyn Lake, 'White Man's Country: The Trans-National History of a National project', *Australian Historical Studies* 34/122, October 2003; 'On Being a White Man, Australia, circa 1900' in Hsu Ming Teo & Richard White (eds), *Cultural History in Australia,* UNSW Press, 2003; 'From Mississippi to Melbourne: the literacy test as a technology of racial exclusion', in Ann Curthoys & Marilyn Lake, *Connected Worlds: history in trans-national perspective*, ANU Press, 2005

2. Lincoln Wright, *APEC: Australia's Pragmatic Asia Policy,* Japan Policy Research Institute, San Francisco Working Paper 8, April 1995

3. See David Marr & Marian Wilkinson, *Dark Victory,* Allen & Unwin, 2003

4. Ann Capling, *All the way with the USA,* UNSW Press, 2005; see also Alison Broinowski, *Howard's War,* Scribe, 2003

5. Kim Humphery, *Shelf Life,* CUP, 1998, p. 36

6. Quoted in Joy Damousi, 'The Filthy American Twang', unpublished paper
7. See Richard Waterhouse, 'Popular Culture', in Philip & Roger Bell, Americanization and Australia, UNSW Press, 1998, pp. 46–7
8. Marion Maddox, God Under Howard, Allen & Unwin, 2005
9. Philip & Roger Bell, Implicated, OUP, Melbourne, 1993, p. 163
10. John Micklethwait & Adrian Wooldridge, The Right Nation, Penguin, NY, 2004, pp. 294–5
11. Donald Horne, The Time of Hope, Angus & Roberston, 1980
12. 'Australia: She'll be right mate—maybe', Time, 24 May 1971
13. Ann Curthoys, Freedom ride: a freedom rider remembers, Allen & Unwin, 2002
14. Anne Summers, 'Sisters out of Step', Independent Monthly, July 1990; Hester Eisenstein, Inside Agitators: Australian Femocrats and the State, Philadelphia Temple University Press, 1996
15. Tim Tembensel, 'International human rights conventions and Australian political debates', Australian Journal of Political Science, 31/1, pp. 7-23
16. Gwenda Tavan, The Long, Slow Death of White Australia, Scribe, 2005
17. See Dorfman & Mattelart, How to read Donald Duck, International General, NY, 1975; Dennis Altman, Global Sex, Chicago University Press, 2001; Joseph Nye, Soft Power, Public Affairs, NY, 2004
18. Mosler & Catley, America and Americans in Australia op. cit., p. 130
19. Richard Waterhouse argues that the US has influenced Australian sport across the board. See his Public Pleasures, Public Leisure, Longman, 1995, pp. 229–30
20. Tony Mitchell, 'The new corroboree', Meanjin, 65/1, 2006
21. Reported in George Megalogenis, The Longest Decade, Scribe, 2006
22. Julian Cribb, 'Show them what you do', Higher Education Supplement, The Australian, 11 January 2006
23. Dennis Altman, Paper Ambassadors, Angus & Robertson, 1991
24. Statement by the Postmaster General, House of Representatives, 21 August 1913

Chapter 2

1. George Megalogenis, 'After the house party ends', Weekend Australian, 18 February 2006
2. John Birmingham, 'So happy we could scream', The Monthly, May 2005, pp. 22-3
3. Don Aitkin, What Was it All For? The reshaping of Australia, Allen & Unwin, 2005
4. Kelly, The End of Certainty, op. cit., p. 62

5. George Megalogenis, 'Government by default', *Weekend Australian,* 4 February 2006
6. On the growth of home schooling, see James Campbell, 'Paranoia and the Breakdown of the Public in American and Australian Schooling Discourse', unpublished paper
7. See Capling, *All the Way with the USA,* op. cit., pp. 60-3
8. Brad Norington, 'My path from bowser boy to IR reform' Interview with John Howard, *Weekend Australian,* 25 February 2006
9. Michael Pusey, *The Experience of Middle Australia,* Cambridge University Press, 2003
10. Ibid, p. 182
11. Ibid, p. 119-21
12. Mark Davis, 'We're not so mean after all', *Weekend Australian Financial Review,* 13 April 2006
13. Robert O'Sullivan, 'Creating Moral Panic: Australian Outrage Radio' in Cryle & Hillier (eds), *Consent and Consensus,* API Network, Curtin University, 2005, pp. 117-34
14. Howard quoted by Carol Johnson, 'Anti-Elitist Discourse in Australia' in Sawer & Hindess, *Us and Them: anti-elitism in Australia,* API Network, 2004
15. For views from the right see Katherine Betts, *The Great Divide,* Duffy & Snellgrove, 1999; Paul Sheehan, *Among the Barbarians,* Random House, 1998. For the response from the left see Robert Manne, *The Barren Years,* Text,2001; David McKnight, *Beyond Right and Left,* Allen & Unwin, 2005
16. See Geoffrey Blainey, 'Drawing up a balance sheet of our history', *Quadrant* 37, July/August 1993, pp. 10-15
17. See Stuart Macintyre, *The History Wars,* Melbourne University Press 2003, pp. 134-6
18. Daniel Ziffer, 'Hearing Voices', *Green Guide, The Age,* 16 March 2006, p. 8
19. See Carla Lipsig, 'Return to the Dark Ages', *The Age,* 11 October 2005; Dirk den Hartog, 'The American IR Model', *The Age,* 5 December 2005
20. Louise Walsh in 'Imagining Australia in 25 Years', *The Age,* 4 February 2004

Chapter 3
1. On Family First, see Haydon Manning & John Warhurst, 'The old and new politics of Religion' in M. Simms & J. Warhurst, *Mortgage Nation: the 2004 Australian Election,* API Network, Perth 2005, pp. 266–70; Amanda Lohrey, *Voting for Jesus,* Quarterly Essay 22, Black Inc, 2006, pp. 44-7
2. Thus Tamas Pataki begins his essay 'Against Religion' with Costello's visit

to Hillsong, *Australian Book Review,* February 2006

3. Richard Florida, *The Rise of the Creative Class,* Pluto 2003, pp. 1–3

4. Marian Maddox, *God Under Howard,* op. cit., p. 200

5. David Burchell, *Western Horizon,* Scribe, 2003, p. 115

6. See Mark Western & Bruce Tranter, 'Are postmaterialists engaged citizens?' in S.Wilson et al., *Australian Social Attitudes,* UNSW Press, 2005, pp. 82–100

7. Irene Webley, 'Women Who Want to be Women' in Marian Sawer (ed.), *Australia and the New Right,* Allen & Unwin, 1982, p. 148

8. David Fawcett, House of Representatives Grievance Debate, 10 October 2005

9. Elizabeth Hill, 'Howard's Choice: the ideology and politics of work and family policy 1996–2006', www.australianreview.net/digest/2006/hill.html

10. See Michael Robinson, 'The road to recovery from drug use: or is it the road to more addiction?' On Line Opinion [www.onlineopinion.com.au] 20 September 2004

11. 'Not Yet Equal', Report of the VGLRL Same Sex Relationships Survey, Melbourne, July 2005

12. There is a copious literature on that response: see Paul Sendziuk, *Learning to Trust,* UNSW Press, 2003, and the bibliography in that book

13. John Warhurst, *Religion and Politics in the Howard Decade,* ANU, March 2006

14. David Marr, *The High Price of Heaven,* Allen & Unwin, 1999, p. xiii

15. See Louis DeSipio & Rodolfo O. de la Garza, 'Making Them Us' in Freeman & Jupp (eds), *Nations of Immigrants,* OUP, 1992, pp. 202-16

16. Alan Ryan, 'A plague on both houses', *Times Literary Supplement,* 21 May 1993

17. See Gibson, McAllister & Swenson, 'The politics of race and immigration in Australia', *Ethnic and Race Studies* 25, 5 September 2002, pp. 823–44

18. Peter Coleman quoted in *The Australian,* 23 March 2006

19. Danna Vale, 'My comments were clumsy', *The Age,* 25 February 2006

Chapter 4

1. See Murray Goot, 'Distrustful, Disenchanted and Disengaged? Polled Opinion on Politics, Politicians and the Parties: A Historical Perspective', in David Burchell & Andrew Leigh (eds), *The Prince's New Clothes: why do Australians dislike their politicians?* UNSW Press, 2002, pp. 9–46

2. See A. Vromen, 'People try to put us down: participatory citizenship of Generation X', *Australian Journal of Political Science,* 3/1, pp. 78–99

3. Josh Gordon, 'MPs warned on self-interest', *The Age,* 3 November 2005

4. Dennis Shanahan, 'Family planning neuters Joyce', *Weekend Australian*, 10 December 2005

5. Shaun Carney, 'The end of responsibility', *The Age*, 11 February 2006

6. Stephen Mills, *The New Machine Men*, Penguin 1986, p. 2

7. Elaine Thompson, 'Political Culture', in *Americanization and Australia*, op. cit., pp. 116–7

8. Carol Johnson, 'The ideological contest' in *Mortgage Nation*, op. cit., p. 48

9. Sally Young, *The Persuaders*, Pluto, 2004, p. 135

10. See James Walter, *The Ministers' Minders*, OUP, 1986

11. See Paul Kelly, *Re-thinking Australian Governance—the Howard Legacy*, ASSA occasional paper, Canberra, 4, 2005, p. 14

12. See Chilla Bulbeck, 'Stifling Freedom of Thought in the Information Age?' *Dialogue* (ASSA Canberra) 24 1/2005, 38–48

13. Judith Brett, *Relaxed and Comfortable*, Quarterly Essay 19, Black Inc, 2005, p. iv

14. Judith Brett, 'John Howard's Legacy', unpublished paper, Canberra, 4 March 2006

15. See Leach, Stokes & Ward, *The Rise and Fall of One Nation*, University of Queensland Press, 2000

16. Geoff Strong, 'A little piece of Tuscany', *The Age*, 22 October 2005

17. See Sean Scalmer, 'Searching for the Inspirationals', *Overland* 180, Spring 2005, pp. 5-9

18. James Walter, 'Aussie Battler, or Worldly Opportunist?' *Australian Universities Review*, 46/2, 2004, p. 8

19. Bob Birrell, Ernest Healy & Lyle Allan, 'Labor's Shrinking Constituency' *People and Place*, 13/2, 2005. For a more technical discussion of the persistence of social structural influences on voting, see David Charnock, 'Post-war changes in the influence of social structure on Australian voting', *Australian Journal of Political Science*, 40/3, September 2005, pp. 343–56

20. See, for example, Thomas Frank, *What's the Matter with Kansas?* Metropolitan, NY, 2004

21. Guy Rundle, 'Notes after "the settlement"' *Arena* 77, June–July 2005, p. 7

22. Dennis Altman, *Rehearsals for Change*, republished by API Network, Curtin University, 2004

Chapter 5

1. See Murray Goot, 'Distrustful, Disenchanted and Disengaged? op. cit.; Judith Brett & Anthony Moran, *Ordinary People's Politics: Australians talk about life, politics and the future of their country*, Pluto, 2006